ALSO BY JUNE SPRIGG

By Shaker Hands

1 9 7 5

THIS IS A BORZOI BOOK
PUBLISHED IN NEW YORK
BY ALFRED A. KNOPF

Domestick Beings

Domestick Beings

ILLUSTRATED,

ANNOTATED,

AND

SELECTED

BY

June Sprigg

ALFRED A. KNOPF

NEW YORK   1984

This is a Borzoi Book published by Alfred A. Knopf, Inc.

Copyright © 1984 by June Sprigg

All rights reserved under International and Pan-American Copyright Conventions.

Published in the United States by Alfred A. Knopf, Inc., New York,

and simultaneously in Canada by Random House of Canada Limited, Toronto.

Distributed by Random House, Inc., New York.

Library of Congress Cataloging in Publication Data

Sprigg, June.   Domestick beings.

1. Women—United States—Biography.

2. Rural women—United States—Biography.

3. Home economics—United States—History—18th century.

4. Diaries. I. Title.

HQ1418.S65   1983   305.4′2′0922   83-47774

ISBN 0-394-40289-8

Manufactured in the United States of America

First Edition

Attend to the ADVICE of
thy MOTHER.

for

Dorothy

Sprigg

I hope I may Live to Spend my time better And have Beter Imployment for my Pen for I must be Scrabling when Leasure time tho I find But very Little time Now. Sometimes after our people is gone to Bed I get my Pen for I Dont know how to Content myself without writeing Something.

Jemima Condict, age 20   West Orange, New Jersey   1774

So long
as a scrap
of paper remains,
I shall keep
scribbling.

Abby May, age 24
Ballston Spa, New York
1800 June 23

I shall write whilst I am on Board when ever I can catch a quiet time, it is an amusement to me, reading tires me, work I do sometimes. But when there is no writing there is less pleasure in working.

Abigail Adams, age 39   Aboard ship on the Atlantic   1784 July 6

Contents

DOMESTICK BEINGS

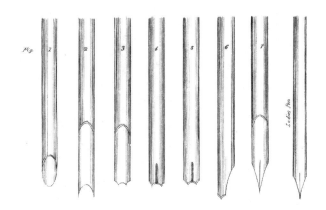

There were not many "female scribblers" in America in the years before 1800. Half of this country's women, or thereabouts, could not write at all, even to sign their names. Of those who could, by no means all had the inclination to write anything as ambitious as a diary or extended correspondence. Fewer still had the gift of expressing themselves so clearly and distinctively that their personalities are preserved in their pages.

This book is about seven who did—seven women whose words convey, with spirit, the experience of their lives in late 18th-century America. They are a personal selection, not a representative one. They did not speak for all women in America, although their attitudes were doubtless shared by many of their friends and neighbors. We have no way to know how typical each was, and it's best to remember that each spoke for herself.

A midwife in Maine, a spinster, a schoolgirl, a farm wife, a young invalid, a President's wife, a farmer's daughter—their lives were diverse, but all had the feeling that something of themselves was worth recording on paper. They shared more than an urge to scribble. Each considered her primary responsibility to be marriage, the business of motherhood, and domestic concerns—in sum, "housewifery". The plot summary each was handed at birth as a woman was the same; what made their stories different was the way each found to write in the details.

But there are surprises here, as well. Many of them, in addition to their household chores, had jobs outside the home—spinning, weaving, sewing, cooking, nursing, or teaching—for income as well as personal satisfaction.

Some of them questioned the desirability of marriage, although there was no really attractive alternative. Finally, there were demands for improvements in women's education and, simultaneously, glimmerings of the conflict to come: that women, once educated, someday might not be content to stay at home.

Amusing, poignant, eloquent, angry, independent, and always refreshingly real, their comments on all these topics, and more, are here. The words are the scribblers' own; the patchwork is mine. Consider it a conversation, if you will, a time for remembering, for laughing, for consoling, for arguing. In its way, this book is a scribbling of my own. If it occasionally reflects the opinions of this twentieth-century scribbler, I simply say with Amelia Simmons,

> The candor of the American Ladies is solicitously intreated by the Authoress, as she is circumscribed in her knowledge, this being an original work in this country. Should any future editions appear, she hopes to render it more valuable.
>
> *American Cookery,* 1796

My aunt Deming gives her love to you and says it is this morning 12 years since she had the pleasure of congratulating papa and you on the birth of your scribbling daughter. She hopes if I live 12 years longer that I shall write and do everything better than can be expected in the *past* 12.

Nanny Green Winslow, age 12   Boston   1771 November 29

Anna Green Winslow

In 1770 ten-year-old Anna Green Winslow said goodbye to her family in Cumberland, Nova Scotia, and sailed off to Boston for schooling in her parents' old hometown. Her father, Joshua, a military man, had moved to Canada because of loyalty to the Crown. "Nanny Green," as she called herself, was named for her mother, Anna Green, and had two little brothers, Johnny and George.

In Boston, Nanny Green attended dancing and sewing schools and stayed with her aunts and their families. Aunts Elizabeth Winslow and Sara Deming were both around fifty; the younger aunt, Elizabeth Storer, was closer to Nanny Green's own mother in age. Like many schoolgirls, Nanny Green kept a daily journal, which she sent home at intervals to acquaint her family with her activities—a cheerful round of lessons, chores, parties, visits, and sermons at the Old South Church. Nanny Green's fine handwriting and orthography reflect her enthusiasm for "scribbling," and her gentle humor recalls the amusement this "whimsical child" brought to her aunts.

Doctr Anderson came up to Day from Schenectady ... he says, he has not doubt I shall be intirely restor'd to Health— and you can have no idea how handsome he looks when he says so ... I have even sometimes thought, Old [Dr.] Pearsons had a pleasing look when he assured me, I should be well— by the bye I never believed him.

Abby May, 24   Ballston Spa, New York   1800 June

Abigail May

In early summer 1800, a new guest checked into the hotel in Ballston Spa, New York, not far from Saratoga Springs. Twenty-four-year-old Abigail May (or Abby, as she was known) had come all the way from Boston to spend the summer seeking a cure for her ailing health in the mineral springs. With Abby were her mother, also named Abigail, and her little brother George. Back home in Boston were her father, John, a respected and well-do-to colonel, and the rest of the ten May children.

Away from the bustle of Boston and her younger brothers and sisters, the summer days stretched long among the pines as Abby settled into a routine of treatment and quiet pastimes. For entertainment the guests played games, had dances, and took walks in the village and surrounding woods. Abby, who loved books and serious conversation, amused herself by writing a long journal for her cousin and adopted sister Lucretia, two years older and a close confidante. The grace of Abby's hand and thought underscore the ability of this bright, sensitive young woman.

Spent the Whole afternoon with my friends that Came from
the West Branch . . . They told me there was young men
Plenty there for me But I thought I was In no hurry for a
husband at Present. And if I was I thought it was too far to go
upon uncertaintys. So I Concluded to Stay where I was & I
Believe I shant Repent it. A Husband or Not, for I am best
of in this spot.

Jemima Condict, age 20   West Orange, New Jersey   1774 October

Jemima Condict

In 1772, when she was seventeen, Jemima Condict took it into her head to start a diary. Unlike
Nanny Green Winslow and Abby May, who had their travels and other new experiences to
write home about, Jemima wrote simply about home and her close-at-hand world in a small
mountain community not far from Orange, New Jersey. Her father, Daniel, was a farmer and
deacon in the local Presbyterian church; her mother, Ruth, took care of the family's eight
children, a responsibility that Jemima, as third oldest, shared.

Like other country diarists, Jemima recorded her chores and Sunday sermons. But she
also used her diary to explore thoughts about marriage, a topic of understandable consequence
to women her age. Although Jemima's wayward spelling and punctuation point to a simple
education, her lively candor and irrepressible spirit show that Jemima questioned the world
around her.

God only knows there is no Person in the world who loves Company more than me ... how it come about that others and all the world was in Possession of children and friends and a hous and homes while I was so od as to sit here alone?

Aunt Bek Dickinson, age 49   Hatfield, Massachusetts   1787 August 13 & 20

Rebecca Dickinson

Rebecca Dickinson was born in 1738, the first child of Moses and Anna Dickinson. Five other children followed, who in turn grew up, married, and had families of their own. But not Rebecca. By the time she was in her forties, Rebecca (or "Aunt Bek," as she became known) had made a living for herself alone in the small town of Hatfield in western Massachusetts. She supported herself by working as a seamstress and for company had her sister and brother-in-law Billings, who ran the local inn. Bek also had occasional care of her elderly mother.

Bek was writing a private diary by her early thirties, but we know only portions from 1787 to 1795. Like Jemima Condict, Aunt Bek used her diary to record neighborhood events, but, more important, she, like Jemima, confided her deepest feelings on marriage and life as a woman alone. In plain words and with heartfelt emotion, Bek's diary touches a universal chord.

I was called at the 6th hour this morn, to see Mrs. Walker at the Hook. Shee was sprigh about the house till 11. Was safe delivered at 12h. and 15m. of a fine son.

Martha Ballard, age 55   Augusta, Maine   1790 March 11

Martha Ballard

Like Aunt Bek Dickinson, Martha Ballard had a profession—she was a midwife and nurse in the small settlement of Augusta in what eventually became the state of Maine. She delivered almost one thousand babies in over thirty years of practice that began in 1778.

But Martha was also a wife, mother, and grandmother more than forty times over. She began her medical career when she was in her early forties, when her six surviving children ranged in age from newborn to over twenty. Her husband, Ephraim, was a land surveyor whose business took him off for months at a time into the wilderness; her sons had trades in woodworking and sawmilling. Martha's large family was a joy to her (with the occasional exception of son Jonathan, whose temper was a trial to even this most patient mother). Her youngest daughters, Hannah and Dolly, and her youngest child, Ephraim, were special in her life.

For almost thirty years Martha made regular note of her activities. Martha's journal was more than a record of neighborhood and household events—it was a memorandum of her prescriptions and treatments. It was also a useful record of birth dates, which the community consulted from time to time. Martha never ventured far or experienced much novelty, but her dedication and warm concern are evident in her steady, homely prose.

O, I am tired almost to death waiteing on visseters. My feet ach as if the bones was laid bare. Not one day's rest have I had this weeke. I have no time to take care of my cloths or even to think my thoughts. Did ever poore creature lead such a life before.

Molly Cooper, age 54   Oyster Bay, Long Island   1769 January 7

Mary Wright Cooper

Poor Molly Cooper—not much ever went right in her life. Born Mary Wright in Oyster Bay, Long Island ("Molly" was her nickname), she was married at age fourteen to Joseph Cooper, bore six children, and was a grandmother at thirty-seven. Molly spent most of her time and energy on farm and household chores and the work of putting up overnight guests; on Sundays she found release in the zeal of the New Light Baptist Church.

Molly began her diary in 1768, when she was in her mid-fifties, and continued it for at least five years. No doubt it helped her to unburden her misery in its pages, for it reads like a litany of complaint.

I am sometimes quite discouraged from writing. So many vessels are taken, that there is Little chance of a Letters reaching your Hands. That I meet with so few returns is a circumstance that lies heavy at my Heart. If this finds its way to you, it will go by the Alliance. By her I have wrote before, she has not yet saild, and I love to amuse myself with my pen . . .

Abigail Adams, age 34   Braintree, Massachusetts   1778 December 27

Abigail Smith Adams

Alone of the scribblers, Abigail Adams needs no introduction. As the wife of the second president and the mother of the sixth, her place in history is assured. But Abigail in her own right is the most exciting spokeswoman of her day. Abigail was a writer, and her ability to capture a mood or to convey a scene on paper matched the extraordinary opportunities life afforded her.

Abigail, the second daughter of William and Elizabeth Smith of Weymouth, Massachusetts, married the young lawyer John Adams just before her twentieth birthday. They had four surviving children. Life for Abigail centered on home and family for the next twenty years; her correspondence with John, separated from the family by politics, is well known. That changed, however, in 1784, when Abigail sailed to Europe to join her ambassador husband just before she turned forty. Her letters from England and France to her sister Mary remain a sparkling glimpse of older nations through Yankee eyes. Upon their return to America and for the rest of her life, Abigail continued to reflect, share, argue, and communicate in letters to family and friends. Her intelligent, articulate comments provide a colorful, thoughtful look at this unusually gifted woman and her times.

I think I write to you every Day. Shall not I make my Letters very cheep; don't you light your pipe with them? I care not if you do, tis a pleasure to me to write, yet I wonder I write to you with so little restraint, for as a critick I fear you more than any other person on Earth, and tis the only character, in which I ever did, or ever will fear you. What say you?

Abigail Smith, age 19   Weymouth, Massachusetts   1764 April 16

. . . I really think that your Letters are much better worth preserving than mine.

John Adams
1776 June 2

But really my journal is quite a different affair from what I expected—habituated to the fire side—and very unused to travelling I concluded it requir'd only the means to commence travelling and elegant writing would follow of course—but I now find to my very great mortification—that a very pleasant journey—has produced a very stupid journal.

Abby May, age 24   Ballston Spa, New York   1800 June 9

Mr. Hunt call'd in to visit us just after we rose from diner; he ask'd me, whether I had heard from my papa & mamma, since I wrote 'em. He was answer'd, no sir, it would be strange if I had, because I had been writing to 'em today, & indeed so I did every day ... He laugh'd & call'd me Newsmonger, & said I was a daily advertiser. He added, that he did not doubt but my journals afforded much entertainment & would be a future benefit &c. Here is a fine compliment for me mamma.

Nanny Green Winslow, age 12   Boston   1772 March 21

THE Place OF A MOTHER & A MISTRESS

Naturally, family and home matters were of great interest to the scribblers. Like most American women in the late eighteenth century, they experienced (or anticipated) marriage in their teens or twenties followed by the birth of children every year or two for the rest of their childbearing years. Large families—six or seven surviving children—were the rule.

As a girl on the brink of adolescence, Nanny Green Winslow was far from thoughts of marriage or motherhood; nothing in her letters home suggests that she was even interested in boys. She did mention weddings, however, as did most of the scribblers. Two weeks after one ceremony, she and her aunts made the traditional wedding visit to the groom and bride; the latter dressed for the event (in Nanny Green's somewhat inexplicable report) in a white satin "night gound."

Abby May and Jemima Condict were both of an age to give serious consideration to marriage. At nineteen, Jemima found her friends urging her to find a husband and her mother asking questions about whether she planned to marry. At twenty-five, Abby was already near the age when still being single suggested a lifetime of spinsterhood. Surprisingly, both young women professed no hurry to wed.

Abby's poor health was undoubtedly a major factor in her situation. Though she was popular and enjoyed the attentions of a circle of "beaux" while convalescing at the spa, Abby must have understood that marriage and (inevitably) motherhood required a vigor that she did not possess. She seemed to accept her lot, and yet it was hard to resign herself completely. Even while denying the possibility of any future with him, Abby was clearly attracted to the young doctor who attended her. "I am continually pester'd about the young Physician," she confided to Lucretia, "so much is said of him when he is away, that when he comes, I cant if I Die, help my Cheeks Glowing . . . and I sometimes fear the good man himself will suspect, the warmth of my Gratitude has kindled another passion in my heart." And yet the situation seemed hopeless. "I wish in my heart he was ninety years old," concluded Abby wistfully.

Jemima also found herself preoccupied with thoughts about men. Despite offers from would-be suitors, Jemima declared a vigorous, comical disdain for marriage, gleefully "scaring off" her pursuers while proclaiming the benefits of independence. The real problem, however, was that Jemima had fallen in love with her cousin, Aaron Harrison. Marriage between near relations had been common throughout most of the eighteenth century, partly because families tended to settle and stay in one area. Abby May's parents were first cousins, both surnamed May. Molly Cooper's daughter Esther married her first cousin, Simon Cooper. But by the end of the century, such matches had begun to raise eyebrows.

Neither Abby nor Jemima seriously disputed the value of marriage, but their occasional wisecracks made the point that it was better to remain unmarried than to marry the wrong man—an attitude echoed by the other scribblers, including Aunt Bek Dickinson, who knew firsthand what a lifetime of spinsterhood was all about.

It was to Aunt Bek above all else lonely. Extremely sensitive to comments, especially from married women, Bek was also frequently hurt by thoughtless questions. During a visit to her married sister in Bennington, Vermont, Bek was "thunderstruck" by a woman who asked her if she were sorry she had not married when she was young. Bek was so overcome by the woman's insensitivity that she went to bed crying and was called "an od being as ever lived" by her sisters, who didn't know the cause of her unhappiness. The incident so distressed Bek that she cut short her visit and returned gratefully home to Hatfield where there were no nosy strangers to ask painful questions.

We're not sure why Aunt Bek didn't marry. Cryptic comments in her diary hint of a hope extinguished in youth, perhaps an unfulfilled courtship. We know that Aunt Bek had (and refused) at least one offer early in her life, from Squire Phelps, who she said "knew too little of himself." Perhaps the difference in their ages—he was twenty-two years her senior—had not appealed to her. And, at the time she was writing her diary, she turned down a doctor from a nearby town, though she was obviously moved by his offer. At age forty-nine, Aunt Bek was too old for motherhood and children, the natural complement to marriage. It could be that, no longer able to have the family she so keenly wanted, Bek felt that a husband alone wasn't worth it. "I really believe there will alwais be a bar in the way," she sighed.

The attitude that Abby, Jemima, and Aunt Bek all expressed—that it was better to be married than single, but better to be single than unhappily wed—was echoed by the scribblers who were married, and by American women in general. Americans in the early years of the republic took pride in the fact that they married by choice, not by aristocratic prearrangement as in Europe. Since marriages were expected to last, choosing a partner was a matter of serious responsibility and consideration of the long-term consequences. Women in America were not as a rule told whom to marry; they made up their own minds. A good choice meant a future of relative happiness, while a bad one spelled disaster. Coping with the consequences of their choices was something that Martha Ballard, Molly Cooper, and Abigail Adams knew from years of personal experience.

We know the least about Martha's marriage because she had so little to say about her husband, Ephraim, whom she called "Mr. Ballard." Whatever praise or complaints she had, Martha didn't put them on paper, simply noting his comings and goings and the gradual passage of anniversaries. By 1785, when she was writing the first diary we have from her hand, they had been married thirty-one years. Martha was nineteen when they wed, Ephraim ten years her senior. At twenty-one, she was the mother of a son, their first-born. By age thirty, she had five young children, ages nine to newborn; she eventually gave birth to nine children.

Though Martha was mum on her marriage, the thanks she gave for her husband's safe return from extended surveying trips, coupled with her obvious delight in their large circle of children and grandchildren (over fifty in all), suggests that Martha and Mr. Ballard spent their fifty-seven years together in a peaceful partnership.

Molly Cooper's situation was different on two counts. She had plenty to say about her husband, Joseph, for one thing, and what she said makes it clear that their partnership was anything but peaceful. By the time Molly was writing the earliest entries known to us, she and

"Dade" had been joined in marriage (perhaps "locked" is a better word) for forty years. Molly was married a few days past her fourteenth birthday, an exceptionally young age even for the early eighteenth century; the groom was twenty-three. Over the next thirty years Molly bore six children.

While all we have is Molly's side of the story, their life together was one of mutual misery. Joseph's behavior (as reported by Molly) ranged from thoughtless to cruel. In spite of their wretched marriage, however, Joseph and Molly stayed together. For them, as for other Americans at the time, separation was not an acceptable alternative, for moral and economic reasons. We don't know what drove their daughter Esther to leave her husband (and cousin) Simon and come back home, but we do know the impact on Esther was devastating. According to Molly, she sometimes cried all day.

Ironically, it was separation that caused the biggest strain in Abigail Adams's marriage. She and John, ten years her senior, married in 1764 when Abigail was nineteen. In the first ten years of their marriage Abigail bore five children. The second decade of their marriage saw John so often and so long away from home that Abigail virtually raised the children and ran the household on her own. She once likened her situation to that of a widow. Prevented from living together for prolonged periods over many years because of the demands of political life, Abigail and John kept their marriage intact by writing. Their correspondence *was* the relationship. Of all the scribblers, it was Abigail who created the most revealing portrait of marriage: the dependence, the jealousies, the hurts, the irritations, the strength, the love.

Their marriage was unusual for reasons other than prolonged separation. It was extraordinarily close, despite absences and grievances. At a time when most women regarded other women and not their husbands as their closest confidantes (perhaps feeling a bond that has diminished with the merging of men's and women's spheres), Abigail considered John her "dearest friend."

⊙　　⊙　　⊚

If there was a common plaint in the comments of the scribblers, it was that a woman's happiness depended absolutely on her husband and that women had no real recourse if things went awry. Yet, the scribblers did not seem to think there was any other way. The attitude that women were subordinate was too entrenched, and too strongly sanctioned by the courts and the church, to allow the scribblers to pursue the radical notion that men and women might expect equal treatment under the law.

Abigail Adams alone suggested that things might be different, in fact should be different. Her directive to John to "remember the Ladies" in establishing new legal codes is now famous as a rallying cry for women's equal rights.

For all her political progressiveness regarding women, however, Abigail did not question the basic role of womanhood accepted and practiced by the other scribblers. "I consider it as an indispensable requisite, that every American wife should herself know how to order and regulate her family; how to govern her domestics, and train up her children," she wrote near the end of her life. "For this purpose, the all-wise Creator made woman an help-meet for man, and she who fails in these duties does not answer the end of her creation."

May God prolong the lives and happiness of the new made pare. May she fill the place of a mother and a mistress to the acceptance of the great Parent of the universe. May the children committed to her parential care, be obedient and ready to receive her good council at all times, and may the God of peace delight to dwell with them, Amen.

Martha Ballard, age 64   Augusta, Maine   1799 November 13

Went up to my Sister ogdens and there was a house full of people ... & there was the new maried Couple ... they tell me he Cryd When he was maried at which I Dont a bit Wonder for I think twas anuf to make the poor fellow bellow if he had his wits about him, for I am shure She Can Beat him.

Jemima Condict, age 20   West Orange, New Jersey   1775

This afternoon is invited the wedners of asa wells of this town who is to be married to bets Smith of Whately   it is agreed by all Peopel there never was a Copel married with so Poor a Prospect of gaining a livelyhood but who knows the fates of men.

Aunt Bek Dickinson, age 49   Hatfield, Massachusetts   1787 November 3

I had some Discourse with Mr. Chandler. He asked me why I
Did not marry   I told him I want in no hurry. Well Said he
I wish I was maried to you. I told him he would Soon wish
himself on maried agin. Why So? Because says I you will find
that I am a crose ill contrived Pese of Stuf   I told him that I
would advise all the men to remain as they was for the women
was Bad & the men so much worse that It was a wonder if
they agreed. So I scard the poor fellow & he is gone.

Jemima Condict, age 20   West Orange, New Jersey   1774

This morning
was more lonesome
than a Cat.

Aunt Bek Dickinson, age 49
Hatfield, Massachusetts
1787 September 5

Being full of thoughts about What to Do as I have this year
Past. Sometimes I think I will Serting Bid him farewell forever
... they tell me they dont think it is a right thing; and it is
forbid &c ... I turned it off with a Laugh & Said What a fool
am I, I talk as if I was going to marry a Cousin ... I Could
wish with all my heart I New the Right way & Could be made
To Chuse it; but if it be rong Then What a fool was I While
yong to Place my mind on such a one as a Cousin,
its very true.

Jemima Condict, age 20   West Orange, New Jersey   1775

How sad the sight to see a woman singel above fifty and not
merried   something is the matter   She is come for a husband
haveing no luck in her own land but why does these foolish
thoughts come   dont happyness lie wholly in the mind?

Aunt Bek Dickinson, age 50   Hatfield, Massachusetts   1788 September

Tis almost 14 years
since we were united,
but not more than half
that time have we
had the happiness
of living together.

Abigail Adams, age 32
Braintree, Massachusetts
1777 August 5

Yesterday was here on a visit doctor gun of montigue a visit
dessined for me . . . he appears more agreable than I Could
think of   He would doe if he was the right one but I never
Shall change my name . . . tho I have no home may it be on
my mind that this week I have had the offer of one.

Aunt Bek Dickinson, age 50   Hatfield, Massachusetts   1788 October 3

This day Is forty years sinc I left my father's house and come
here, and here have I seene littel els but harde labour and
sorrow, crosses of every kind. I think in every respect the state
of my affairs is more than forty times worse than when I came
here first, except that I am nearer the desierered haven.

Molly Cooper, age 55   Oyster Bay, Long Island   1769 July 13

I long to hear that you have declared an independancy—and
by the way in the new Code of Laws which I suppose it will
be necessary for you to make I desire you would Remember
the Ladies, and be more generous and favourable to them than
your ancestors. Do not put such unlimited power into the
hands of the Husbands. Remember all Men would be tyrants
if they could.

Abigail Adams, age 31   Braintree, Massachusetts   1776 March 31

Jonathan here; informed me Mrs. Peter Jones is very unwell,
ocationed by her husband's ill usage and keeping her in the
seller barefoot. O the wretch; he deserves severe punishment.

Martha Ballard, age 57   Augusta, Maine   1792 June 21

There was a woman who had been exceeding Prosprous in the world asked me whether I was not Sorry that I did not marry when I was young . . . my reply to her was that my affairs might be in a worse Situation.

Aunt Bek Dickinson, age 50   Hatfield, Massachusetts   1788 September 22

The lady was Mrs Poor—Meriam Fullerton—the gay sprightly Meriam Fullerton that was—but oh! how alter'd— she looks dull, dejected, in short like a *married woman* . . . Oh, I'll never be married, if such sower looks comes of matrimony.

Abby May, age 20   Portland, Maine   1796 August

Good Night
Friend of my Heart,
companion of my youth—
Husband and Lover—
Angels watch thy Repose.

Abigail Adams, age 32
Braintree, Massachusetts
1777 September 17

Alass! How many snow banks devide thee and me and my warmest wishes to see thee will not melt one of them . . . My daily thoughts and Nightly Slumbers visit thee, and thine. I feel gratified with the imagination at the close of the Day in seeing the little flock round you inquiring when Mamma will come home—as they often do for thee in thy absence.

Abigail Adams, age 29   Weymouth, Massachusetts   1773 December 30

I have the pleasure to inform you that last Night Mrs. Smith got to Bed with an other fine Boy. We could have all wisht it had been a Girl, but rest satisfied with the sex as it [is] a very fine large handsome Boy and both Mother and child are well.

Abigail Adams, age 45   Richmond Hill, New York   1790 August 8

My aunt stuck a white sattan pincushin for Mrs. Waters. On one side, is a planthorn with flowers, on the reverse, just under the border are, on one side stuck these words, Josiah Waters, then follows on the end, Dec[r] 1771, on the next side & end are the words, Welcome little Stranger.

Nanny Green Winslow, age 12   Boston   1771 December 30

A severe storm of rain. I was called at 1h. p.m. . . . by Ebenezer Hewen. Crost the river in their boat. A great sea a going. We got safe over, then sett out for Mr. Hewen's. I crost a stream on the way on floting logs and got safe over. Wonderfull is the goodness of providence. I then proseeded on my journey. Went beyond Hainses when a lardg tree blew up by the roots before me; which caused my horse to spring back, and my life was spared. Great and marvilous are they spareing mercies, O God. I was asisted over the fallen tree by Mr. Hains. Went on. Soon came to a stream; the bridge was gone. Mr. Hewen took the rains, waided thro and led the horse. Asisted by the same allmighty power, I got safe thro, and arived unhurt. Mrs. Hewen safe delivered at 10h. evening, of a daughter. My cloak was burnt while there so that it is not wareable. I received 8 shillings.

Martha Ballard, age 54   Augusta, Maine   1789 April 24

I have been alone this day, since my children left me. Have felt very gloomy. May my mind be resined to thy will in all things.

Martha Ballard, age 63   Augusta, Maine   1798 July 23

She has been a favirite of fortin   She was well merried
has had fore Children the number So many Pitch upon as
being a Proper number.

Aunt Bek Dickinson, age 49   Hatfield, Massachusetts   1788 February

Called to see Mrs. Hains; shee was safe delivered at the 10th
hour, evening, of a fine daughter. I tarried all night; my
patients cleverly; this is her 11th child, 6th daughter.

Martha Ballard, age 55   Augusta, Maine   1790 September 15

Daughter Pollard and two of her children, Sally, Martha
and James came here forenoon. It is as a cordial to have a
child come to see me.

Martha Ballard, age 75   Augusta, Maine   1810 March 20

David Pattee's wife
departed this life the 4th
(of this month) in child bed.
Shee left 12 children
to mourn the loss.

Martha Ballard, age 54
Augusta, Maine
1789 December 8

My patient was safe delivered
at 4h. morn, of a fine daughter—
her first born. This is the
750th case I have had.

Martha Ballard, age 63
Augusta, Maine
1798 November 24

. . . I hear also
that the Widow Fitch
has had a son. . . .

Martha Ballard, age 51
Augusta, Maine
1786 June 29

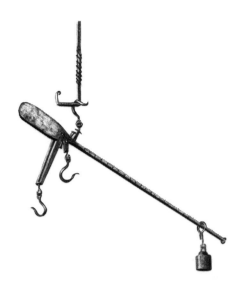

I was called at 5h. p.m., to see the wife of George Thomas. She was safe delivered at 7 of a son, which weighed more than the lite side of Mr. Densmore's stillyards would weigh.

Martha Ballard, age 62   Augusta, Maine   1797 March 22

Sunday. I have felt very unwell, but have had the noise of children out of 5 familys to bear; some fighting, some playing, and not a little profanity has been performed.

Martha Ballard, age 69   Augusta, Maine   1804 April 14

I was called at the rising of the sun to Sarah White, shee being in travail with her forth child, and is yet unmarried.

Martha Ballard, age 54
Augusta, Maine
1789 June 20

Sabbath. A fine clear still day. Ester, her dade, and Rachel go to church and I have the blessing to be quite alone, without any body greate or small.

Molly Cooper, age 54   Oyster Bay, Long Island   1768 October 23

I congratulate you and my dear Neice upon the late happy event in your Family. Can you really believe that you are a Grandmamma?

Abigail Adams, age 45   Richmond Hill, New York   1790 April 3

ABOVE

Wrought-iron steelyards.
They were useful around the house for weighing flour, coffee, salt—or babies.

OPPOSITE

An unusual pine swinging cradle, c. 1800.

I shall wish to hear from Mrs. Norton as soon as she gets to Bed. I think you told me that she expected this month and Sister Shaw too. It is really a foolish Business to begin after so many years, a second crop.

Abigail Adams, age 45   New York   1790 March 15

DOMESTICK BEINGS

Because the scribblers' lives revolved around home and family, they wrote a great deal about housework, or what the eighteenth century called "house-wifery." As women, their concerns included preparing food and making clothing, keeping the house clean and comfortable, and attending to the family's health. The scribblers didn't make the distinction we do between "going to work" and "staying home"—home *was* the workplace.

We don't know much about the actual homes of the scribblers, since most of these are long gone; the few that survive have been much changed and, without their original furnishings and inhabitants, are hard to interpret. Still, we can make some generalizations. The scribblers and their families were accustomed to more people in fewer and smaller rooms than is usual today. Besides members of the family, each home customarily housed servants, visitors, and boarders. And people had fewer possessions—most museum settings today show too many and too precious objects for a realistic view of ordinary eighteenth-century life. Closets were seldom found in houses. Instead, the whole dwelling, from cellar to garret, was used for active storage. Key rooms included the kitchen and parlor; people slept and stored household things in chambers.

Houses were colder and darker than we're apt to expect, and more plagued with vermin. Firewood and candles, even when provided at home, were costly, and used thriftily. Indoor plumbing meant a chamber pot; the warm-weather alternative was the "necessary," outdoors. Outbuildings for other purposes, including cooking and washing, in season, were standard in most homes.

The furnishings themselves varied in each scribbler's home. Furniture styles depended on the area's traditions and on the scribbler's budget. The styles we call "Queen Anne" and "Chippendale" (after an English monarch and English cabinetmaker) were the most modern and fashionable available. The highest-priced furniture was elaborately carved and made of imported mahogany. Ordinary furniture was made locally of local woods like pine or maple in simple designs and often decorated and protected with paint. Silver was out of the question for all but the most prosperous households; pewter was the scribblers' equivalent of our stainless steel. Brass and copper were similarly prized. Wood and earthenware or stoneware were the commonest household materials, much like our plastic.

Textiles for the home were generally fewer, and more often homemade. Carpets were rare, and most commonly woven of scraps and rags. Upholstered furniture was much less common than it is today. Seats in plain wooden chairs were usually made of wood splint or twisted rush. Though comparatively scarce, household textiles like carpets and curtains were likely to be made at home from purchased fabrics, not homespun—England's trade with America in commercial fabrics was large and extensive. Wallpaper was rare and expensive; more common were plain whitewashed walls or painted wood paneling. Floors were plain pine boards; the wide boards and random widths we value today in old houses were not necessarily prized by their original owners, who probably thought nice uniformly sized boards were more desirable. The architectural style we call Federal, with its large windows and neo-classical decoration, was the style of the future.

We can make other generalizations about family life and housework, too. Domestic help was far more common in the scribblers' day than it is now. Slavery, though thought of as a southern institution, was well established in the Northeast. And young women without other career opportunities found domestic work a practical source of income, especially before marriage. We know that at least five of the seven scribblers in this book had household help (only Jemima Condict and Aunt Bek Dickinson do not mention paid or slave assistance).

While each of the scribblers, as women, shared the same basic household responsibilities, the actual workloads each experienced varied with individual income, family size, and other factors. Besides, each had her own reaction to the housework that was part of all women's lives.

As a young girl, Nanny Green Winslow's domestic chores were relatively light, particularly as she was both a student and a guest in her aunts' homes in Boston. Like most comfortably settled Bostonians, Aunt Deming had help, in the person of Lucinda, a black woman born in Africa and bought by Aunt Deming as a child of about seven. Much later when Aunt Deming died, Lucinda was given her freedom. Because of these circumstances, it is likely that Nanny Green was spared the ordinary household chores of sweeping, scrubbing, washing and ironing, and polishing brass and pewter.

Abby May was similarly spared the usual chores because she was a guest at a fully staffed resort spa; at home her delicate health and servant help probably exempted her from heavy housekeeping as well. At the spa, Roby, a "good little girl," slept in a cotbed in Abby's chamber and made the bed and swept for Abby. She also assisted in dressing Abby. Abby's family friends, the Westerns, brought a servant man and a black woman with them during their stay at Ballston Spa. While at the spa, Abby had very little to do in the way of domestic work and filled her time with writing, reading, games, walking, and other diversions instead.

Jemima Condict's experience was more typical of young unmarried women her age. As a farmer's daughter and one of eight children, Jemima was undoubtedly capable of running the household by the time she was in her teens. Although she didn't write much about the work of housekeeping, we know that Jemima could cook and weave; presumably she could tackle other household chores as well.

As an unmarried woman, Aunt Bek Dickinson provided the sole income in her household. And, unlike married women of her age with grown daughters to help around the house, Aunt Bek had to do all her household work by herself. But she never mentioned housekeeping in her diary.

As mature mistresses of their households, Martha Ballard, Molly Cooper, and Abigail Adams kept detailed records of their housekeeping practice. Their experience was shared by most other American women in the Northeast before 1800.

Martha Ballard's diary records almost thirty years of her household work. By the date of the earliest entries we have from her hand, Martha at fifty was just about through raising her children. Only the youngest, six-year-old Ephraim, and her two teenaged girls, Dolly and

Hannah, remained at home. The girls were a big help to Martha, already well into her later life career as a midwife and nurse.

In addition, Martha consistently had help from hired girls. In 1785 she hired Hannah Barton to do the kitchen work; four years later, Mrs. Wall's daughter came to work as an apprentice for six weeks; six years after that, she dismissed Elizabeth Taylor for bad manners, and so on.

The marriages of her daughters increased the burden of household work for Martha. One month after Hannah married and "went to housekeeping," taking Dolly with her for assistance and company, Martha noted that she did the first washing she had done without help in several years. Other housekeeping chores that Martha mentioned over the years included soap-making, candle-dipping, chopping wood, plucking feathers for bedding, and scrubbing (in addition to all her work with textiles and meals).

Molly Cooper, who also lived on a small farm, shared many of the same chores. Molly also had help; in 1755 her family owned four slaves, whom she called "our peapel." Nonetheless, Molly complained constantly that she was overworked, typically up late or all night doing some chore, frequently "dirty and distressed," always behind with the laundry. For some reason, probably for a little additional income, Molly took in overnight lodgers, a common occupation for women at a time when hotels were few and far between. (Martha also mentioned accommodating visitors overnight.) Molly cooked and cleaned for her family *and* her "visse-tors" and despised it. In August 1769 she wailed to her diary that Ben Hildrith came with two men and their two dogs, which they kept at the table and in the bedroom. "They did nothing but drink themselves drunk all the day long," Molly added in disgust, "and sent for more rum." Two days later, they set sail, to her "great Joy," and she desired that she might never see them again. "I greately dread the cleaning of the hous after this detested gang," was Molly's final shot.

As far as housekeeping chores went, Abigail Adams as a young woman experienced much the same situation as did Martha Ballard and Molly Cooper. When she and John married, their first home was an old wood-framed house on a small farm not far from her girlhood home. Like other farmwives, Abigail was in charge of chores including most of the work directly connected with raising and preserving food. She had help—Judah, a black woman servant—sent by her mother-in-law. Abigail had been raised with both servants and slaves (her parents had a slave man and woman). Throughout her life, however, Abigail recognized the conflict between political ideals of freedom and the institution of slavery. "I wish most sincerely there was not a Slave in the province," she wrote at one point later in her life. "It allways appeard a most iniquitous Scheme to me—fight ourselfs for what we are daily robbing and plundering from those who have as good a right to freedom as we have." In later years Abigail's domestic help was hired, not slave.

What made Abigail's housekeeping experience different from that of Martha's or Molly's as time went by, however, was the extraordinary amount of extra work caused by moving and maintaining several households. In the politically troubled years before the Revolution, the young family moved several times from the farm to Boston and back again. Abigail finally settled on the farm in Braintree and spent the next decade there.

Nothing about life on the farm prepared Abigail for housekeeping in France where she joined John in 1784. In Auteuil, near Paris, she suddenly found herself mistress of a thirty-room mansion; and she was aghast to learn that French custom dictated the hiring of eight servants in addition to the two she had brought from home. When they moved to London the next year, she was further dismayed to find that a four-story townhouse required a personal maid, butler, housemaid, coachman, cook, kitchen maid, and two footmen. All this went against her New England grain, and she always maintained that American servants were simply harder workers than their European counterparts.

Later, back in America, John's political career kept Abigail moving from household to household, to rented homes in New York and Philadelphia, to the brand-new President's house in Washington, D.C., and always back home to Massachusetts, where they owned a house they named "Peacefield," which she remodeled and filled with furnishings shipped home from

Europe. That home, in Quincy, is now open to the public. Like other mistresses of large estates, Abigail found that servant help did not exempt her from the responsibilities of housewifery; it simply changed the nature of her involvement from direct work to supervision. There were times when it seemed to Abigail that the gains were questionable.

Looking back at the scribblers from the viewpoint of a very different age, it might be tempting to assume that all of the scribblers regarded their homemaking lot as burdensome. And yet, only Molly Cooper voiced constant dissatisfaction. The others had good days and bad, but accepted their work and the amount of it as women's proper occupation.

Women you know Sir are considered as Domestick Beings, and altho they inherit an Eaquel Share of curiosity with the other Sex ... have generally speaking obstacles sufficient to prevent their Roving ...

Abigail Adams, age 26   Braintree, Massachusetts   1771 April 20

I have been picking wool till 11h. A woman's work is never done, as the song says, and happy she whos strength holds out to the end of the rais.

Martha Ballard, age 60   Augusta, Maine   1795 November 26

An eighteenth-century kitchen cupboard. Slots in the shelves hold an impressive number of spoons.

Simon Cooper
brought home
a dish rack
and a chest.

Molly Cooper, age 54
Oyster Bay, Long Island
1769 April 27

Well orderd home is my chief delight, and the affectionate domestick wife with the Relative Duties which accompany that character my highest ambition.

Abigail Adams, age 38   Braintree, Massachusetts   1783 June 20

I got Safe home & Glad on it too for I Like home the Best & tis a great mercy that I have Such a home to go to. The old saying is home is home, Let it be ever So homely & I think So, tho I Count Not my fathers a homely Home Nither would I have you think so my friends.

Jemima Condict, age 20   West Orange, New Jersey   1775

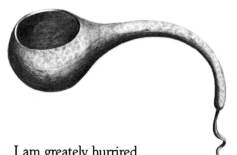

I am greately hurrired cookeing and cleaning my bedroom. Very unwell and tired almost to death.

Molly Cooper, age 54
Oyster Bay, Long Island
1768 November 12

The hail cesses this morning and floods of rain pores down with frightfull gusts of wind which blew away parte of the kitchen. We have hardly a dry place in the house. I suffered much this day with the wet and cold, and am up all night.

Molly Cooper, age 57   Oyster Bay, Long Island   1771 March 10

I have possession of my Aunts chamber in which you know is a very conveniant pretty closet with a window which looks into her flower Garden. In this closet are a number of Book Shelves, which are but poorly furnished, however I have a pretty little desk or cabinet here where I write all my Letters and keep my papers unmollested by any one. I do not covet my Neighbours Goods, but I should like to be the owner of such conveniances. I always had a fancy for a closet with a window which I could more peculiarly call my own.

Abigail Adams, age 31   Boston   1776 August 29

This House is twice as large as our meeting House. I believe the great Hall is as Bigg. I am sure tis twice as long ... But this House is built for ages to come ... I had much rather live in the house at Philadelphia. Not one room or chamber is finished of the whole. It is habitable by fires in every part, thirteen of which we are obliged to keep daily, or sleep in wet & damp places ...

We have not the least fence, yard, or other convenience, without, and the great unfinished audience-room I make a drying-room of, to hang up the clothes in.

Abigail Adams, age 55   Washington, D.C., The White House   1800 November 21

ABOVE

A long-handled wrought-iron flesh fork and ladle. The bowl of the ladle is brass.

OPPOSITE

An eighteenth-century stoneware jug in the common onion-bulb shape; three drinking mugs, made of wood, gray stoneware, and reddish-brown earthenware; and a hollow dried gourd used as a dipper or a measure.

I have a pretty good Housekeeper, a tolerable footman, a midling cook, an indifferent steward and a vixen of a House maid, but she has done much better laterly, since she finds that the housekeeper will be mistress below stairs.

Abigail Adams, age 44   Richmond Hill, New York   1789 November 3

I paid Elizabeth Taylor six shillings for what work she has
done for me, and dismist her, and she went away about 2h. p.m.
I am determined not to pay girls any more for ill manners.

Martha Ballard, age 60   Augusta, Maine   1795 December 19

Come to this old hous to sleep . . . I desire to be thankfull
that God has Provided So good a house for me.

Aunt Bek Dickinson, age 49   Hatfield, Massachusetts   1788 June 15

Ester gon to
town to get
a lamp and oil.

Molly Cooper, age 56
Oyster Bay, Long Island
1771 March 20

Was called to see Mrs. Wasson; I find her as well as could
be expected, but of the mind shee cannot take care of her
infant at home—a stupid afair I think—but shee must
do as shee pleases.

Martha Ballard, age 56   Augusta, Maine   1791 November 16

The snow is near gone in the street before us, & mud supplys
the place thereof . . . what was last week a pond is to-day a
quag, thro' which I got safe however, & if aunt had known it
was so bad, she sais she would not have sent me, but I neither
wet my feet, nor drabled my clothes. . . .

Nanny Green Winslow, age 12   Boston   1772 April 1

I am much distrest. No clothes irond, freted and tired almost
to death and forst to stay at home.

Molly Cooper, age 54   Oyster Bay, Long Island   1769 May 7

I have made 28 doz.
dipt candles.

Martha Ballard, age 53
Augusta, Maine
1788 April 12

You inquire of me how I like paris? Why they tell me I am no judge, for that I have not seen it yet. One thing I know, & that is, that I have smelt it . . . it is the very dirtyest place I ever saw . . . the floors I abhor, made of red tile in the shape of mrs Quincys floor cloth tile. These floors by no means bear water, so that the method of cleaning them is to have them waxt & then a man Servant with foot Brushes drives round your room dancing here & there like a merry Andrew . . . & the stairs which you have to assent to get into the family appartments are so dirty that I have been obliged to hold up my Cloaths as tho I was passing through a cow yard.

Abigail Adams, age 39   Auteuil, France   1784 September 5

. . . I have got some clean cloths on thro mercy. Very littel done to clean the house.

Molly Cooper, age 54   Oyster Bay, Long Island   1769 December 15

And do you know where I can get a steady body? A cook is of the most concequence. I must not have one who will be put out of humour by company comeing in unexpectedly. She must be willing upon washing & Ironing days to assist in the after part of the day to fold cloaths & to help Iron if necessary, to keep every thing clean and neat in her department.

Abigail Adams, age 55   Philadelphia   1800 April 26

ABOVE

A tin box that hung from the ceiling to keep candles safe from mice and rats.

OPPOSITE

Two small oil-burning iron "betty lamps."

I rose early, put on a kettle of water to boil; then milkt and got breakfast, and did my washing; then went to the spring for water.

Martha Ballard, age 65   Augusta, Maine   1800 May 19

The family have been *scrubbing* the house as they phrase it,
and really tis almost a float—they pour on the water, and then
scrub with brooms, scampering about the wet floor barefoot—
I wonder they dont catch their deaths.

Abby May, age 24   Ballston Spa, New York   1800 May 26

It is Crysmas Day.
I have done a
fortnit's wash....

Martha Ballard, age 72
Augusta, Maine
1807 December 25

... the first time we were all able to go upon deck, I sum-
moned my own Man Servant, who before had been as sick as
any of us, and sent him down with all the Boys I could mus-
ter, with Scrapers, mops, Brushes, infusions of vinegar &c. and
in a few hours we found there *was* Boards for a floor ... since
which I have taken upon me the whole direction of our cab-
bin, taught the cook to dress his victuals, and have made several puddings with my own hands.

Abigail Adams, age 39   Aboard ship on the Atlantic   1784 July 10

How Poor and low
my Spirits ... Poorer than
a Cat which has been
in a barrel of Sope
and was al over Covered.

Aunt Bek Dickinson, age 49
Hatfield, Massachusetts
1787 October

We are much hurred and have not done cleaning the house.
Oh, it has been a week of greate toile and no comfort or piece
to body or mind.

Molly Cooper, age 55   Oyster Bay, Long Island   1769 May 20

The hoops of my soap barrels broke, and let my soap out. I had
a great fatague in geting it up; lost a good deal.

Martha Ballard, age 60   Augusta, Maine   1795 August 31

I have put my bed into the bedroom; corkt the cracks and hung up sheets to make the rooms more comfortable.

Martha Ballard, age 70   Augusta, Maine   1806 January 22

I was called
to see Mrs. Savage;
tarried all night.
O the flees.

Martha Ballard, age 57
Augusta, Maine
1792 August 17

I am tired almost to death. . . . I am drying and ironing my cloths til allmost brake of day.

Molly Cooper, age 54   Oyster Bay, Long Island   1768 December 24

We are wonderfull dirty and distrest with a grate many things that we don't now where to set.

Molly Cooper, age 56   Oyster Bay, Long Island   1771 February 28

I have been washing the things which were brot from the woods. A dirtyer parsil of cloaths I never saw.

Martha Ballard, age 61   Augusta, Maine   1796 October 19

RIGHT

A small wooden dipper made like a barrel with staves and hoops.

OPPOSITE

A common scrub brush made of peeled birch, and a barrel of the sort used to store pickled pork, sugar, apples, flour, or soap. This one was made with wooden hoops.

An old Indian come here to day that lets fortans and ueses charmes to cure tooth ach and drive away rats.

Molly Cooper, age 55
Oyster Bay, Long Island
1769 August 5

I have so little Time that I can call my own whilst here that I think when I return to Braintree I ought without suffering from any reflections to be able to live retired. On Monday Evenings our House is open to all who please to visit me. On Twesdays my domestick affairs call for me to arrange them & to labour pretty well too, for the Wednesdays dinners which we give every week to the amount of sixteen & 18 persons … On Thursday the replacing & restoring to order occupies my attention. The occasional intercourse of dinning abroad, returning visits &c leaves me very few hours to myself.

Abigail Adams, age 47   Philadelphia   1791 December 18

Mr. Halloway
mended puter
for me.

Martha Ballard, age 51
Augusta, Maine
1786 June 24

A Hundred dollers
goes but a little way
in good furniture.

Abigail Adams, age 45
New York
1790 August 29

So one Day my mother Says to me your father is going to get you a Chest   I told her I should be Glad of one But Would not have her think twas because I thought to Marry. Why Says she Dont you never intend to marry?

Jemima Condict, age 20   West Orange, New Jersey   1775

Ester has freted
most grevously
all day long
about cleaning
the house.

Molly Cooper, age 55
Oyster Bay, Long Island
1769 September 25

I have been at home. Did the
house work ... Drove Densmore's
swine out of the corn, and
mended the fence.

Martha Ballard, age 60
Augusta, Maine
1795 August 27

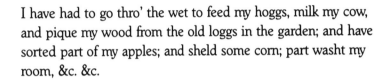

I have had to go thro' the wet to feed my hoggs, milk my cow,
and pique my wood from the old loggs in the garden; and have
sorted part of my apples; and sheld some corn; part washt my
room, &c. &c.

Martha Ballard, age 69   Augusta, Maine   1804 October 24

... Grumblers
there always was
& always
will be.

Abigail Adams, age 45
New York
1790 July 4

I broke old loggs with an old
hough, and brot in the pieces in a
basket; and O how fatagued I was.

Martha Ballard, age 69
Augusta, Maine
1804 October 25

RIGHT
A tall basket made of splints
stripped from an ash log.

OPPOSITE
A common pine six-board chest.

It has beene
a tiresome day to me.
It is now bed time
and I have not had
won minuts rest today.

Molly Cooper, age 54
Oyster Bay, Long Island
1768 November 20

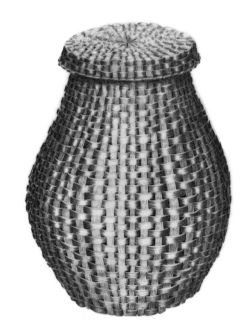

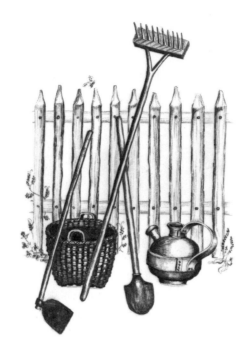

We Are Like to Have a *Plenty*

Food was an important part of the scribblers' everyday experience. Like other Americans, what the scribblers ate depended on what was available locally and on the season of the year. Their concerns were more with preserving food adequately than with preparing elaborate meals. Keeping butter and cheese fresh, minimizing rot in stored fruits and vegetables, keeping meat untainted—these were the main responsibilities. What the scribblers ate was cooked over an open fire or coals on the kitchen hearth, where it was possible to roast, fry, boil, broil, steam, and bake. Oven baking took place less often (and primarily for food in larger quantities) because of the amount of firewood needed. The scribblers grew much of their own food, but when it was more convenient they bought it. There were English cookbooks available, but most of the meals the scribblers cooked and ate were simple and did not require written instructions. The recipes included in this chapter (from *American Cookery*, America's first native cookbook, published by Amelia Simmons in Hartford in 1796) are typical of the methods familiar to the scribblers, although these women did not necessarily own this cookbook or any other.

Nanny Green Winslow had the least responsibility in this department. The meals in her aunts' Boston households were probably prepared by the servants. We assume that Nanny Green did not have to gather eggs, churn butter, weed the kitchen garden, or do any of the other chores required of a farm girl. The few occasions when Nanny Green mentioned eating were parties: she and her girlfriends nibbled on cakes, nuts, and raisins, washed down with wine and punch. The use of alcohol by children was neither uncommon nor considered improper. Besides these few brief references, though, Nanny Green was silent on the subject of food, and not surprisingly so. As writers, she and the other scribblers found no point in discussing food unless it were something special.

Jemima Condict, too, had little to say about meals or food, possibly because in a plain farm household her family did not often have occasion for special treats. She mentioned actual cooking only once, when she helped fix "roast meat & Bakt Podins" for soldiers drilling on a training day. Though she "workd Perdigus hard all Day" she went home at sunset indignant that the cooks "got But Little" of the meal. "I took to my Bed & was Glad when I got there," she grumped, "for upon my word Which you may Believe at this Present Junkture I was tired anuf." We don't know whether Jemima helped with kitchen work regularly or whether her mother or a sister took care of that business. Perhaps she was just not interested in the topic.

As a guest in a resort spa, Abby May of course did not have to bother herself with fixing meals. She simply went down to the dining hall to eat what was served. In spite of her poor health, Abby did take notice of her food. En route to Ballston Spa from Boston, she noted with a sigh for its monotony, that veal was served in every tavern along the way. At the spa, though generally satisfied with her environment, she longed for "Music, Books, Fruits, and Vegetables—these are all strangers to us."

Like most Americans, Abby and her acquaintances took their main dinner meal in the middle of the day and had a light supper or tea in the evening. For one supper she had tart, fruits, and milk. Abby's spirits and appetite perked up considerably on a trip to Lake George, where fresh fish was the specialty. At first, she couldn't bring herself to eat a supper of bass and perch when she learned they were recently caught. She laughed at her sensitivity—"I could not eat any of them after this recommendation . . . tho I know every thing must die before it can be eaten, I hate to have it brought to my rememberance"—and ate mutton, instead. Abby evidently overcame her tender sympathies because soon after she thoroughly enjoyed an island picnic of fresh fish, "cold provisions," and liquor.

Abby was more interested in the dining hall's company than in the food, and she wrote frequently about the characters that amused her. To her dismay, Abby found the tables turned one day when a convention of forty lawyers passed through. "I was absolutely obliged to set down to breakfast in the long room with the batch of lawyers and gents I mention'd," she reported to Lucretia. "I would rather have waited till Christmas for my meal—and indeed said so—however set down I did—wit, and repartee, flew briskly round and I should have been really gratified, if a pleasant companion had been with me—but as it was I found such beauties in my cup and saucer I look'd at nothing else—how like a fool one acts, and feels, in such a situation, while those high and mighty Lords of the Creation as they call themselves will pick their teeth and stare confidently in your face . . ."

Aunt Bek Dickinson chose not to trouble herself with meals. In 1788, she decided to take meals at the nearby tavern owned by her sister Miriam and her brother-in-law. It was a happy change. Instead of dining alone, she sat down at the table every day with fourteen others, delighted to have the companionship. "This is a beautiful Summers Day," she wrote one June morning in 1788, "have just been down to brother billings to breakfast . . . there is the hous where I can injoy my Self, the Company is more than the Provision, how our Comfort depends on the Company that wee keep . . ."

Martha Ballard and Molly Cooper both wrote extensively about food, although their focus as farmwives was mostly on the work involved. Their chores were remarkably similar and probably typical of many other women in similar homes. Both had kitchen gardens and fruit trees; both did butchering work at slaughtering time; both tended poultry. But there were variations in their responsibilities, too. Molly kept bees for honey; Martha made her own cheese at home.

Both women found their workloads and meals shaped by the seasons. In spring they planted vegetables and began to make fresh butter. Martha brewed barrels of beer. In summer they gathered and preserved fruit—strawberries, cherries, and blackberries. Molly had a "water million patch." Over the years Martha mentioned some of her crops: cucumbers, onions, peas, cabbage, potatoes, winter squash, currants, turnips, pumpkins, and many varieties of beans, including string, yellow-eyed, Poland, shell, scarlet, crambury, brown, and hundred-to-one. In this season Molly stayed up late making wine; Martha made pickles. It was also time to kill calves for veal.

In fall, Martha and Molly dried apples; Martha also dried pumpkins, Molly dried pears. In late fall or winter, both rendered lard, stuffed sausages, and made mincemeat for pies after the annual hog slaughter. Martha's son Jonathan brought her venison and moose meat in the winter. Molly salted beef. With the end of winter, Martha helped make maple syrup as the sap began to flow. Then the yearly cycle began once again.

While the Ballard and Cooper households produced most of the food they ate, they also bought supplies. Rum, coffee, tea, sugar, chocolate, molasses, and salt were common imported staples that Martha and Molly mentioned. In addition, on occasion Martha bought preserved pork, cider, smoked herring, and gingerbread. Although Martha did most of her own dairy work, she occasionally bought cheese and butter. Martha and Molly both sold surplus produce as well. Both women sold cherries; the Coopers sold turkeys, potatoes, hogs, and strawberries. Martha did baking for other families from time to time.

The main difference between Martha and Molly was probably the amount of time each spent in the kitchen. Martha had a busy career in midwifery and nursing; her daughters, before their marriages, undoubtedly helped. She also hired girls to help and sometimes specified that their work was "kitchen work." Molly, in contrast, was responsible for all the cooking in her household, which brought her no joy. "Dinner to get and nothing in the house to cook" was one of Molly's most common complaints.

As a young wife on the small farm in Massachusetts, Abigail Adams experienced much the same responsibilities as Martha and Molly. She tended cows, sheep, and chickens, and raised vegetables. When John's career took him away from home for long periods of time, Abigail took over supervision of the field crops and other farming matters traditionally handled by men. Her capability earned his admiration. In 1776 she noted, "We are just now ready to plant, the barly look[s] charmingly, I shall be quite a Farmeriss an other year." John replied: "I think you shine as a Stateswoman, of late as well as a Farmeress. Pray where do you get your Maxims of State, they are very apropos."

With her move to Europe, however, Abigail's role changed. Instead of doing most of the work herself, she directed servants in shopping and preparation—in effect, serving more as a restaurant manager than as a cook, and more as a consumer than a producer. Her new role was typical of well-to-do women in cities or on large estates back in America, too, and Abigail continued it when she and John returned to Philadelphia, New York, and Washington, D.C., ordering produce, meat, and butter from their farm back in Massachusetts because she was sure the quality was better.

Like the other scribblers, Abigail didn't mention specific meals unless they were really noteworthy. As the wife of an ambassador and, later, a President, she enjoyed some very elegant dining, in both the English and French fashion, with multiple courses, exotic foods, and elaborately decorated tables, set with serving dishes arranged in studied symmetry. The other scribblers ate more plainly. The common American diet in the late eighteenth century was based largely on cornmeal bread or mush, salt or fat pork, dried apples, squash, pumpkins, and root vegetables like potatoes, carrots, and turnips, which stored well during the winter.

If the scribblers could peer into our lives as we peer into theirs, we wonder what they might think of our own ways with cooking and food. Certainly the equipment would mystify them (it mystifies some of us). The variety of food and its year-round availability would astonish them. The complexity of an ordinary week's menu would probably impress them—their meals, which took longer on the average to prepare, were simpler as a result, and the lack of variation in a season didn't seem to make much difference. The quantities we have on hand in our cupboards would strike them as woefully small. Their understanding of nutrition was different from ours; vitamins and calories were still concepts of the future.

We are like to have a plenty of sause. I shall fat Beaf and pork enough, make butter and cheesse enough. If I have neither Sugar, molasses, coffe nor Tea I have no right to complain. I can live without any of them and if what I enjoy I can share with my partner and with Liberty, I can sing o be joyfull and sit down content.

Abigail Adams, age 32   Boston   1777 August 22

When I come to this place again I am determined to bring a *decent woman* who understands plain cooking with me. Such a vile low tribe you never was tormented with & I hope never will be ... I have had in the course of 18 months seven, and I firmly believe in the whole Number, not a virtuous woman amongst them all: the most of them drunkards. I recruited with a new one last Monday ... but on thursday got so drunk that she was carried to Bed, and so indecent, that footman, Coachman & all were driven out of the House.

Abigail Adams, age 46   Philadelphia   1791 January 9

*Oval wooden storage boxes
and a variety of herbs.*

How to choose the best in market.

Veal, is soon lost—great care therefore is necessary in
purchasing. Veal bro't to market in panniers, or in carriages, is to
be prefered to that bro't in bags, and flouncing on a sweaty horse.
A Goose, if young, the bill will be yellow, and will have but few
hairs, the bones will crack easily . . . choose one not very fleshy
on the breast, but fat in the rump.

Amelia Simmons, _American Cookery_

Eggs—Clear, thin shell'd, longest oval and sharp ends are best
. . . The best possible method of ascertaining, is to put them into
water, if they lye on their bilge, they are _good_ and _fresh_—if they
bob up an end they are stale, and if they rise they are addled,
proved, and of no use.

Amelia Simmons, _American Cookery_

Colde. O, I am
dirty and tired allmost
to death cooking for
so many peopel, freted
almost to death.

Molly Cooper, age 54
Oyster Bay, Long Island
1769 March 7

I am very busie
and mighty angrey
becaus the cittel is
sent for before I have
don my quinces.

Molly Cooper, age 58
Oyster Bay, Long Island
1772 October 16

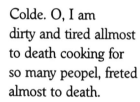

<u>Herbs, useful in Cookery.</u>

<u>Thyme</u>, is good in soups and stuffings.
<u>Sweet Marjoram</u>, is used in Turkeys.
<u>Summer Savory</u>, ditto, and in Sausages and salted Beef, and legs of Pork.
<u>Sage</u>, is used in Cheese and Pork, not generally approved.
<u>Parsley</u>, good in <u>soups</u>, and to <u>garnish roast Beef</u>, excellent with bread and butter in the spring.
<u>Penny Royal</u>, . . . might be more generally cultivated in gardens, and used in cookery and medicines.
<u>Sweet Thyme</u>, is most useful and best approved in cookery.

Amelia Simmons, <u>American Cookery</u>

We proceed to ROOTS and VEGETABLES—<u>and the best cook cannot alter the first quality, they must be good; or the cook will be disappointed.</u>

<u>Potatoes</u>, take rank for universal use, profit and easy acquirement . . .
<u>Parsnips</u>, are a valuable root, cultivated best in rich old grounds, and doubly deep plowed, <u>late sown</u>, they grow thrifty, and are not so prongy; they may be kept any where and any how . . .
<u>Garlicks</u>, tho' used by the French, are better adapted to the uses of medicine than cookery.

Amelia Simmons, <u>American Cookery</u>

. . . Retiring to our own little farm feeding my poultry and improveing my garden has more charms for my fancy, than residing at the court of Saint James's where I seldom meet with characters so innofensive as my Hens and chickings, or minds so well improved as my garden.

*A splint egg basket
and different fowl.*

Abigail Adams, age 43   London   1788 February 26

53

Took care
of my pickles;
put them
into vinegar.

Martha Ballard, age 60
Augusta, Maine
1795 August 27

<u>To pickle Cucumbers.</u>

Let your cucumbers be small, fresh gathered, and free from spots;
then make a pickle of salt and water, strong enough to bear an
egg; boil the pickle and skim it well, and then pour it upon your
cucumbers, and stive them down for twenty four hours; then
strain them out into a cullender, and dry them well with a cloth,
and take the best wine vinegar, with cloves, sliced mace, nutmeg,
white pepper corns, long pepper, and races of ginger, (as much as
you please) boil them up together, then clap the cucumbers in,
with a few vine leaves, and a little salt, and as soon as they begin
to turn their colour, put them into jars, stive them down close,
and when cold, tie on a bladder and leather.

Amelia Simmons, <u>American Cookery</u>

I was mighty angry this morning becaus our peopel did not
bring in the pumkins and they are all frose and spoiled.

Molly Cooper, age 58   Oyster Bay, Long Island   1772 November 18

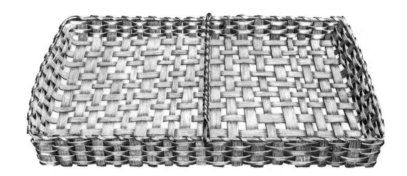

I am forst to
climb the cherre tree
and fetch the bees
down in my a pron.

Molly Cooper, age 59
Oyster Bay, Long Island
1773 June 13

I am drying cheres. Still very greateliy distrest giting dinner.

Molly Cooper, age 55   Oyster Bay, Long Island   1769 July 25

<u>For preserving</u> *Quinces* <u>in Loaf Sugar</u>.

Take a peck of Quinces, put them into a kettle of cold water,
hang them over the fire, boil them till they are soft, then take
them out with a fork, when cold, pair them,
quarter or halve them, if you like; take
their weight of loaf sugar, put into a
bell-metal kettle or sauce pan, with one
quart of water, scald and skim it till it
is very clear, then put in your Quinces,
let them boil in the sirrup for half
an hour, add oranges as before if
you like, then put them in
stone pots for use.

Amelia Simmons, <u>American Cookery</u>

Cheese—*The red smooth, moist coated, and tight pressed, square edged Cheese, are better than white coat, hard rinded, or bilged; the inside should be yellow, and flavored to your taste . . . Deceits are used by salt-petering the out side, or colouring with hemlock, cocumberries, or safron, infused into the milk; the taste of either supercedes every possible evasion.*

Amelia Simmons, American Cookery

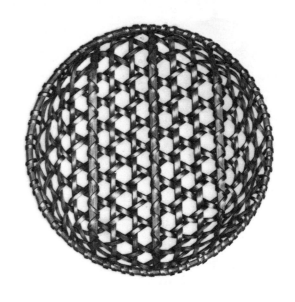

What do you think will become of us. If you will come Home and turn Farmer, I will be a dairy woman.

Abigail Adams, age 32   Braintree, Massachusetts   1777 July 23

I have made a new milk cheese—changed milk with Mrs. Joy. I had my puter can 28 times full in my cheese.

Martha Ballard, age 62
Augusta, Maine
1797 July 19

Nothing remarkabel
except that we had
the heavyest bread
I had ever seene.

Molly Cooper, age 55
Oyster Bay, Long Island
1769 August 29

Another Christmas Cookey.

To three pound flour, sprinkle a tea cup of fine powdered
coriander seed, rub in one pound butter, and one and half pound
sugar, dissolve three tea spoonfuls of pearl ash in a tea cup of
milk, kneed all together well, roll three quarters of an inch thick,
and cut or stamp into shape and size you please, bake slowly
fifteen or twenty minutes; tho' hard and dry at first, if put into an
earthern pot, and dry cellar, or damp room, they will be finer,
softer and better when six months old.

Amelia Simmons, American Cookery

Minced Pies. A Foot Pie—

*Scald neet's feet, and clean well, (grass fed are best) put them
into a large vessel of cold water, which change daily during a
week, then boil the feet till tender, and take away the bones,
when cold, chop fine, to every four pound minced meat—add
one pound of beef suet, and 4 pound apples raw, and a little salt,
chop all together very fine, add one quart of wine, two pound of
stoned raisins, one ounce of cinnamon, one ounce mace, and
sweeten to your taste; make use of paste No. 3—bake three
quarters of an hour.*

Amelia Simmons, *American Cookery*

Snows and blows, but we
are able to make a fire and have
food to eat, which is a great
mercy for which I wish to
thank the Great Doner.

Martha Ballard, age 62
Augusta, Maine
1807 April 1

I have bakt mins
and apple pies.

Martha Ballard, age 70
Augusta, Maine
1805 December 28

Dried Apple Pie.

Take two quarts dried apples, put them into an earthen pot that contains one gallon, fill it with water and set it in a hot oven, adding one handful of cramberries; after baking one hour fill up the pot again with water; when done and the apple cold, strain it, and add thereto the juice of three or four limes, raisins, sugar, orange peel and cinnamon to your taste; lay in paste No. 3.

Amelia Simmons, American Cookery

ABOVE

A rolling, or "paste," pin; a "jagging iron" used to trim and crimp piecrust; and a pie plate.

OPPOSITE

Common kitchen equipment: a built-in oven, a swinging crane, andirons, a flesh fork, a ladle, skewers, a churn, a peel, a kettle, a small standing saucepan, a revolving broiler, and a standing or hanging griddle. Wooden and wrought-iron peels were used to move bread, pies, and other baked goods in and out of the oven, much like a modern pizza shovel.

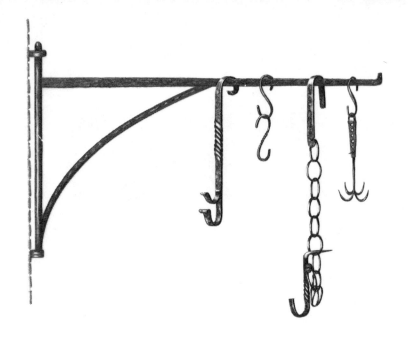

Dined on calves'
head and harslett and
other good things.

Martha Ballard, age 65
Augusta, Maine
1800 December 23

<u>To stuff and roast a Turkey, or Fowl.</u>

One pound soft wheat bread, 3 ounces beef suet, 3 eggs, a little
sweet thyme, sweet marjoram, pepper and salt, and some add a
gill of wine; fill the bird therewith and sew up, hang down to a
steady solid fire, basting frequently with salt and water, and roast
until a steam emits from the breast, put one third of a pound of
butter into the gravy; serve up with boiled onions and cramberry-
sauce, mangoes, pickles or celery.

Amelia Simmons, <u>American Cookery</u>

It is our yearly Thanksgiving. We roasted a goose;
boiled beef, pork and fowls for dinner.

Martha Ballard, age 68   Augusta, Maine   1803 December 1

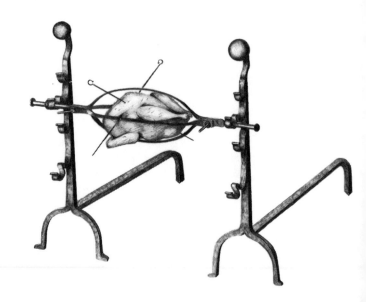

We are very buesy
killing hogs.

Molly Cooper, age 55
Oyster Bay, Long Island
1769 November 23

I have finisht trying
hogg's lard; cut sauches
meet, and done
other matters.

Martha Ballard, age 68
Augusta, Maine
1803 December 30

ON THIS PAGE

A sausage stuffer, a wooden
gutscraper, and a lard press.

OPPOSITE

An iron hearth crane
and adjustable kettle hangers,
and a basket spit and andirons.

I will thank you to make my Bacon for me, and when it is fit
to smoak let Mr. Belcher carry it to the same place he got the
other smoakd at. But I do not want it here. God Willing I
will eat it at Home, & stay not an hour here longer than
duty requires.

Abigail Adams, age 53   Philadelphia   1797 November 28

A Tasty Indian Pudding.
Salt a pint meal, wet with
one quart milk, sweeten and
put into a strong cloth,
brass or bell metal vessel,
stone or earthern pot, secure
from wet and boil 12 hours.

Amelia Simmons, American Cookery

I am more distrest than eaver.
I have dinner to get and nothing
in the house to cook. . . . Dirty
and distressed, I set my self to
make some thing out of littel on.

Molly Cooper, age 55
Oyster Bay, Long Island
1769 September 17

I would have Mrs. Burrel
have some pots to lay
me down some butter . . .
we are an Army of our-
selves, and shall want
a good deal.

Abigail Adams, age 55
Philadelphia
1800 April 17

Diet Bread.
One pound of sugar,
9 eggs, beat for an hour,
add to 14 ounces flour,
spoonful rose water,
one d [itt] o. cinnamon or
coriander, bake quick.

Amelia Simmons, American Cookery

I wish to have our winter Apples, pears, Butter, some cheese, Bacon, Tongue &c all from our own state & what I cannot get from the Farm I would get put up in Boston, such as Hams & Tongues. I mention'd all these things to Mr. Adams, but do not know that he will be attentive about them.

Abigail Adams, age 44   New York   1789 November 1

ON THIS PAGE

A covered kettle and pot hook,
fire tongs and shovel, and a grisset,
for catching meat juices.

OPPOSITE

A long-handled skillet, skewers
(for pinning joints into position for
roasting), a toaster, and a Dutch oven.

To have sweet butter in dog days, and thro' the vegetable
seasons, send stone pots to honest, neat, and trusty dairy people,
and procure it pack'd down in May, and let them be brought in
in the night, or cool rainy morning, covered with a clean cloth
wet in cold water, and partake of no heat from the horse, and set
the pots in the coldest part of your cellar, or in the ice house.—
Some say that May butter thus preserved, will go into the winter
use, better than fall made butter.

Amelia Simmons, <u>American Cookery</u>

We dined on
a fine leg of
corned pork stufft
with green herbs
from our garden.

Martha Ballard, age 51
Augusta, Maine
1786 April 7

I am wondrous dull! you see it, without any hint I imagine—
in Truth I have eaten so heartily of a Veal Pye and Currant
Tart—I can hardly keep my eyes open.

Abby May, age 24   Ballston Spa, New York   1800 June 7

We had a handsome dinner of salt fish pea soup Boil'd fowl
& tongue roast & fry'd Lamb, with a pudding & fruit, this was
a little in the Boston Stile.

Abigail Adams, age 39   London   1784 July 25

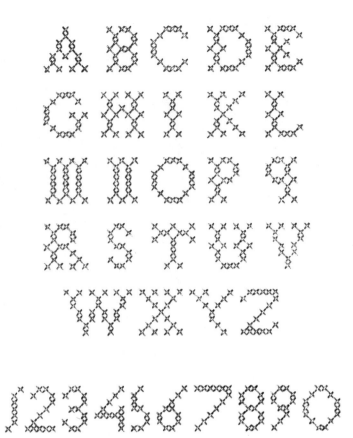

I Seek Wool & Flax

Making and maintaining clothes and household textiles—sheets, towels, coverlets, sacks, and the like—was an important part of women's housekeeping responsibility. Sewing, mending, knitting, cleaning, and pressing were all part of the job. In many households where some or all of the cloth itself was made at home, spinning, weaving, dyeing, and other specialized tasks might be added to the list.

Cloth-making became particularly important during the war, when British yard goods went off the market; women who had bought their fabric for years found themselves limited to homespun, a badge of honor for those who supported the Revolution. Even so, it wasn't usually necessary to produce the cloth start to finish at home. Professional male and female weavers and dyers provided their services for an affordable fee. The scribblers varied in their work with textiles, which was to be expected, given these options and the differences in their ways of life.

Naturally, the scribblers were interested most in their own clothes. By the end of the eighteenth century, imported fabrics were back on the shelf, and women who continued to make linen and woolen cloth at home for everyday wear or household use could buy nice patterned cottons or silks for their best outfits. They could also hire seamstresses or "mantua-makers" to style the gown in the fashionable way.

Like other American women, the scribblers had wardrobes made of several standard items. Outerwear was a gown or two-piece separates of a jacket and skirt or petticoat. Underwear included a shift or full slip, stockings tied at the knee with garters, and a laced corset or stays. Underpants were probably not basic wear. Drawers (with two legs joined at the waist and an open crotch) were just beginning to catch on.

Other basics included caps, aprons, leather or cloth shoes, and large neck handkerchiefs to drape over the shoulders and pin at the bosom. For cold or wet weather there were shawls and cloaks. Other accessories—baglike pockets to tie at the waist, mitts or gloves, hats, fans, jewelry—varied with individual taste and budget, as did each woman's notion of what was in style. Fashions, introduced in the glittering courts of London and Paris, trickled back to America by word-of-mouth or printed fashion-plates. From Boston, New York, Philadelphia, and other cities, news of the latest "modes" filtered out into the smaller towns and farms around. Then as now, high fashion in Paris and Maine was not the same thing.

Training in needlework and interest in clothes began early in a woman's life. Like other young girls, Nanny Green Winslow took care of much of the household sewing and mending. Nanny Green spun, made shirts for her uncle and shifts for herself, and knitted and "new footed" stockings. She mended gloves and handkerchiefs and worked on patchwork for a bed cover. Most everyday needlework was a chore, but some of it was fun—knitting lace or doing "network" for trims.

What Nanny Green liked best was working on clothes—shopping for "ribbins," hats, an ermine trimming for her cloak. Delighted to be in a large stylish city (and anxious to fit in and "look like other folk"), Nanny Green put a great deal of thought and her aunts' money into her wardrobe, which she described in loving detail for her mother back home. Though she was young, Nanny Green even had her hair dressed in the towering bouffant style popular in the late eighteenth century and copied for her family's amusement a "droll figure of a young lady, in or under, which you please, a tasty head Dress" of a similar style from an English print.

Abby May's experience with clothing and needlework was similar to Nanny Green's, although Abby had less to do in the way of practical or "plain sewing" since she was both indisposed and on vacation. Abby kept her hands busy with decorative needlework. She knotted, netted, made tassels and fringes, wove watch chains, did braided hair work, and drew patterns for "Fillagree work for the Ladies" at the spa. She ornamented a handkerchief with a design of oak leaves and acorns as a gift.

Abby also amused herself by observing the fashions of the other women there, and though we don't know what she wore herself, she found herself "not a little scrimpt for clothing," a situation her mother rectified by making a gown and sending a parasol from Boston.

Jemima Condict's experience was different from that of the two city girls. Like many other young women in small towns and farms, Jemima knew how to spin and produce homespun. She was also a weaver, which was less common; the expense of a major piece of equipment like a loom and the technical skill of weaving made it more practical for many women to send their homespun yarn to a professional weaver. Jemima wrote very little about her clothing except to mention a cloak her father bought her—a very special gift—and to note that she spent some time assisting a tailor who visited their house to work on the family's new clothes.

It is probable that Jemima used her weaving abilities for occasional profit. Textile-related work was a respectable, acceptable source of income for women of the working class. As the habitual occupation of unmarried women such work, of course, gave rise to the term "spinster." For Aunt Bek Dickinson, needlework was more than a part of housekeeping, it was a living. "My daily bread depends on my labour," she noted of her career as a gown-maker in 1787, "God has in great mercy this Summer back given me work. He heard my Poor request—and has Sent employ for my hands." Later that year she worried that she was "out of imploy" in the weeks before Thanksgiving, ordinarily a very "hurried" season for her. As a gown-maker Aunt Bek customarily traveled to other people's homes to bring her services to her customers.

As farmwives Martha Ballard and Molly Cooper had as much to do with textile work as they did with food. Both knew firsthand the work of growing flax for linen and raising sheep for wool. Spring was the time to sow flax seed and shear sheep. By midsummer the tall flax plants were ready for harvest and processing into fiber for spinning, a long, complicated procedure involving rotting, braking, swingling, combing, hatcheling, and other tedious chores to separate the woody stalk from the soft inner strands. That work stretched through the year—flax pulled in July might be finished for spinning the next spring.

Wool processing was short and simple, in contrast. The fleeces were washed, picked apart, and sorted by quality of wool, then greased and carded into fluffy cylindrical rolls. Spinning took place year-round as needed, but especially during the winter when it was a good way to keep industrious near the fire. The cycle came to an end and a beginning in mid-winter with the birth of lambs, an event that more than once forced both women to venture forth into a howling winter night.

Though Martha and Molly were familiar with all the steps of wool and linen processing, they most certainly did not handle each step single-handedly. Homespun production was cooperative work. Shearing was men's work. Tending the flax, carding, spinning, and other jobs were shared by women in the household and on occasion by hired or traded help. Martha's teenaged daughters Hannah and Dolly were a big help; they wove, mended, spun, and made clothes.

The same variations in kinds and amounts of labor were true for the rest of the textile operations. Martha and Molly both dyed at home, but Martha also sent cloth to a mill to be colored and pressed. Martha had a loom, which her daughters and several neighborhood women used; Molly sent her yarn to the weaver. Both Martha and Molly had their gowns made by other women. Martha went to Mrs. Densmore and, later, to Dolly. When Molly wanted a new gown, she had Mrs. Weeks come to the house and stay for a couple of days. And both Martha and Molly bought fabric and other notions on occasion, including linen, flannel, cambric, cotton, and thread.

In her diary Martha also wrote about Dolly's experience as a seamstress—at age nineteen, Dolly went for a year to learn tailoring from a neighbor, Mr. Densmore. That Dolly was a seamstress must have made Martha's life easier, since her own career in midwifery left her less time for domestic chores. Before her formal training, Dolly was already accomplished in textile work. She wove and made shirts, stays, and a "rapper" for Hannah. Afterward, she made bonnets, mended, and cut and stitched cloaks, gowns, and waistcoats for neighbors who came to the house.

Still, her mother's list of sewing chores was long. Martha made note in her diary of combing and hatcheling flax, carding cotton, quilting, picking and washing wool, mending, scouring yarn, bleaching linen, cutting rags for rag carpets, and dyeing cloth. Above all, perhaps, she liked to knit and turned out a steady stream of mittens and stockings for her children and grandchildren. On Christmas Eve in 1794, Martha finished a pair of mittens for Ephraim, her fourteen-year-old son, the "first striped ones" she ever knit. It seems that she was pleased.

If Abigail Adams had stayed on the farm, her experience might have resembled that of Martha and Molly. As a girl and young wife, she knew the same traditional skills and seasonal cycles. The changes that life as an ambassador's wife and President's lady brought, however, substantially altered her work with the needle.

For one thing, although she boasted of her patriot's pride in homespun during the war, she didn't spend much of her time producing it afterward. Abigail was not only near Boston's shops, but she also sold imported yard goods herself at one point in her life. In 1780 during John's second sojourn abroad, she had him send ribbons, lace, cloth, and silk handkerchiefs, which she in turn sold to a wartime market eager for niceties.

Later, when she joined her husband in London, her consciousness of their role as representatives of the new nation helped shape her standards for fashionable dress, which to Abigail's mind must be well-made but not extravagant. Dismissing the "foil and tincel" of English ladies and the Queen, who was "stiff with diamonds," Abigail chose to exemplify the "American neatness" she admired in others of her country. Her mantuamaker cut and stitched accordingly. Abigail sent fashion news home to her female relatives and continued to do so when she returned to America's own style centers, New York and Philadelphia.

Today we don't have much except the scribblers' words to tell us about their needlework. The actual articles are long gone, the sheets and towels turned into rags (and perhaps later into fine rag paper), the clothes mended and altered and handed on and mended and altered again until they, too, faded into rags and disappeared.

But what does survive tells a story of its own. Aunt Bek's hands not only stitched and seamed and scribbled in her diary, they embroidered fanciful, flowing grapevines, pears, pinks, and clover blossoms. Three of her embroidered coverlets, worked in shades of indigo blue crewel wool, are known today. One is most mysterious. Aunt Bek worked it in 1765, when she was twenty-seven, along with another young woman, Polly Wright. We don't know why Bek chose to embroider a large, full-rigged ship on it or what the cross-stitched inscription above the ship means:

```
FOAWTWA      COGVIUSA
        M    D
REBEKAH      DICKINSON
  POLLY      WRIGHT
        L    D
    1 7      6 5
```

The portions of Aunt Bek's diary that survive give no clue about this coverlet and make no mention of this colorful aspect of her needlework.

But the coverlets themselves tell us something that Aunt Bek and all the scribblers knew. Of all a woman's housekeeping duties, needlework alone could produce something that endured. More than a necessary chore, it could provide an outlet for creativity and an opportunity to create something prized and saved, if not for all time, then at least as long as it could be used. For many women who were not "scribblers," needlework was the only such chance.

I seek wool and flax and can work willingly with my Hands,
and tho my Household are not cloathed with fine linnen nor
scarlet, they are cloathed with what is perhaps full as Honorary,
the plain and decent manufactory of my own family, and
tho I do not abound, I am not in want.

Abigail Adams, age 32   Braintree, Massachusetts   1777 April 17

Rose in the morning tho not very early and Went to weaving
yet not very willingly for tho I Love that yet it likes not me and
I am in the Mind that I never shall be well as Long
as I Weave.

Jemima Condict, age 17   West Orange, New Jersey   1772 May 20

*A crewel-work design.
The cow and large flower,
drawn in ink, were
never stitched.*

This is a day to Be remembered. I am so distrest and afraid
that som body will come here about my perplext affiars that I
went out of the house about nine a'clok, in the morng and sat
by the path side sewing til just be fore sundown.

Molly Cooper, age 57   Oyster Bay, Long Island   1771 May 4

I am heshling
flacks.

Molly Cooper, age 55
Oyster Bay, Long Island
1769 November 15

Frances began
to combe wool.

Molly Cooper, age 58
Oyster Bay, Long Island
1772 August 3

I have been doing
things about house,
and tended my
thread to whiten.

Martha Ballard, age 62
Augusta, Maine
1797 October 30

I have been
carding tow.

Martha Ballard, age 62
Augusta, Maine
1797 March 24

I have hatcheled
14 lbs. flax from
the swingle.

Martha Ballard, age 60
Augusta, Maine
1795 March 16

Polle gon
to carre yarne
to the weaver.

Molly Cooper, age 58
Oyster Bay, Long Island
1773 April 19

Mended me
a handkerchief,
and made
a night cap.

Martha Ballard, age 72
Augusta, Maine
1807 November 18

Cyrus shearing
our sheep.

Martha Ballard, age 58
Augusta, Maine
1793 May 29

Mr. Hamlen
made me a present
of a quill wheal ...

Martha Ballard, age 56
Augusta, Maine
1792 January 18

Dolly spun
me yarn for
candle wicks.

Martha Ballard, age 62
Augusta, Maine
1797 February 21

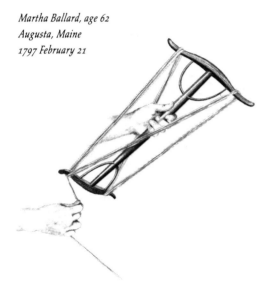

My cousin Sally reeled off a 10 knot skane of yarn today. My valentine was an old country plow-joger. The yarn was of my spinning. Aunt says it will do for filling. Aunt also says niece is a whimsical child.

Nanny Green Winslow, age 12   Boston   1772 February 14

ON THIS PAGE

A niddy-noddy, for measuring yarn or thread, and a quill wheel, for filling shuttle bobbins.

OPPOSITE

Flax blossom and seeds, and two ways of preparing wool: carding, by pulling the fibers between the short wire teeth of cards, and combing, by drawing fleece through the long iron spike of a worsted comb.

Any body that sees this may see that I have wrote nonsense but Aunt says, I have been a very good girl to day about my work however—I think this day's work may be called a piece meal for in the first place I sew'd on the bosom of unkle's shirt, mended two pair of gloves, mended for the wash two handkerchiefs, (one cambrick) sewed on half a border of a lawn apron of aunts, read part of the xxi^st chapter of Exodous, & a story in the Mother's gift.

Nanny Green Winslow, age 12   Boston   1772 March 9

My aunt gives her love to you & directs me to tell you that she tho't my piece of linnin would have made me a dozen of shifts but she could cut no more than ten out of it. There is some left, but not enough for another. Nine of them are finish'd wash'd & iron'd; & the other would have been long since done if my fingers had not been sore.

Nanny Green Winslow, age 12   Boston   1772 March 17

Yesterday see the Widow Patte graves of Pitsfield   She began the world with me   we went together to learn the trade of gown making which has been of unspeakable advantages to me but of no Servis to her. She married a man Seven and thirty years older than her Self has Six Children living.

Aunt Bek Dickinson, age 49   Hatfield, Massachusetts   1787 September 26

. . . altho' I can drive the goos quill a bit, I cannot so well manage the needle.

Nanny Green Winslow, age 12
Boston
1772 February 10

Dolly went to Mr. Densmore's to learn the taylor's art. I wish her success and happiness.

Martha Ballard, age 56   Augusta, Maine   1791 November 15

I have finisht a pair hose for John Town. It is the 17th pair I have knit since this year commenced.

Martha Ballard, age 65   Augusta, Maine   1800 March 29

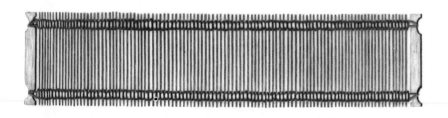

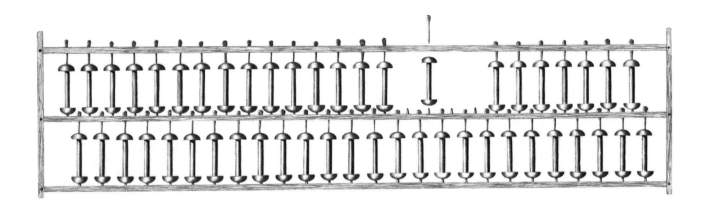

I feel concerned least your cloaths should go to rags having nobody to take any care of you in your long absence, and then you have not with you a proper change for the Seasons. However you must do the best you can. I have a suit of homespun for you whenever you return.

Abigail Adams, age 29   Braintree, Massachusetts   1776 June 3

I hope aunt wont let me wear the black hatt with the red Dominie—for the people will ask me what I have got to sell as I go along street if I do, or, how the folk at New guinie do? Dear mamma, you dont know the fation here—I beg to look like other folk. You dont know what a stir would be made in sudbury street, were I to make my appearance there in my red Dominie & black Hatt.

Nanny Green Winslow, age 11   Boston   1771 November 30

Detachable pockets were tied around the waist and worn under the skirt. The common pair opposite was made of white linen. Weaving equipment: a reed (opposite) used to gauge the width and fineness of the weave; the scarne (above) held spools for ease in warping the loom.

I should certainly use some Red Broad cloth if I could come at it, for red cloth Cloaks are all the mode, trim'd with white furs. This is much more rational than to wear only a shawl in winter.

Abigail Adams, age 55   Philadelphia   1799 December 4

To amuse you then, my dear niece, I will give you an account of the dress of the ladies at the ball . . . not all their blaze of diamonds, set off with Parisian rouge, can match the blooming health, the sparkling eye, and modest deportment of the dear girls of my native land . . . "And pray," say you, "how were my aunt and cousin dressed?" If it will gratify you to know, you shall hear. Your aunt, then, wore a full-dress court cap without the lappets, in which was a wreath of white flowers, and blue sheafs, two black and blue flat feathers (which cost her half a guinea a-piece, but that you need not tell of), three pearl pins, bought for Court, and a pair of pearl ear-rings, the cost of them—no matter what; less than diamonds, however. A sapphire blue demi-saison with a satin stripe, sack and petticoat trimmed with a broad black lace; crape flounce, &c; leaves made of blue ribbon, and trimmed with white floss; wreaths of black velvet ribbon spotted with steel beads, which are much in fashion, and brought to such perfection as to resemble diamonds; white ribbon also in the Vandyke style, made up of the trimming, which looked very elegant; a full dress handkerchief, and a bouquet of roses. "Full gay, I think, for my *aunt.*" That is true, Lucy, but nobody is old in Europe. I was seated next the Duchess of Bedford, who had a scarlet satin sack and coat, with a cushion full of diamonds, for hair she has none, and is *but seventy-six* . . .

Abigail Adams, age 41   London   1786 April 2

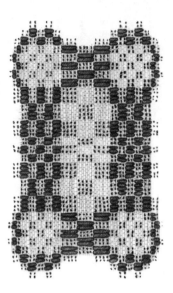

. . . to be out of fashion, is more criminal than to be seen in a state of Nature to which the parisians are not averse.

Abigail Adams, age 39
Auteuil, France
1784 September 5

My cloak & bonnett are really very handsome, & so they had need be. For they cost an amasing sight of money, not quite £45   tho' Aunt Suky said, that she suppos'd Aunt Deming would be frighted out of her Wits at the money it cost. I have got *one* covering, by the cost, that is genteel, & I like it much myself.

Nanny Green Winslow, age 11   Boston   1772 January 4

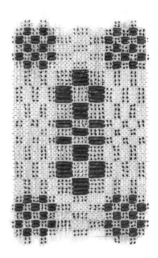

Mrs F—— dresses very smart—and I expect has a stock of clothes than will enable them to wear different dresses every day—they brought no less than 7 trunks ... Yesterday she was habited in a spotted muslin trim'd round with green velvet and Lace—a band of the same round her head, and a chip chapeau with a painted handkerchief and Wreath of roses upon it—A pearl comb &cc—she is so handsome one cannot help gazing at her.

Abby May, age 24   Ballston Spa, New York   1800 July 13

My dear father went to town & Came home at Night & gave me a fine Present; it was a Long Cloak a Present indeed Such a one as I did not Deserve; But you cant think how I felt When he gave it to me   I was Both glad & sorry. I was glad of the Present yet I was Sorry I had not bin more Deserving & that I had Not Bin more thankfull & behavd myself better in the Servis of So Kind a father; & I wanted my sister to have one.

Jemima Condict, age 19   West Orange, New Jersey   1775 January 11

ABOVE

A detail from a professionally woven reversible overshot coverlet made of white linen thread and indigo woolen yarn.

OPPOSITE

The same detail in reverse.

This minute I have receiv'd my queen's night cap from Miss Caty Vans—we like it. Aunt says, that if the materials it is made of were more substantial than gauze, it might serve occasionally to hold any thing mesur'd by an 1-2 peck, but it is just as it should be, & very decent. But I got into one of my frolicks, upon sight of the Cap.

Nanny Green Winslow, age 12   Boston   1772 March 28

I had my HEDDUS roll on, aunt Storer said it ought to be made less, Aunt Deming said it ought not to be made at all. It makes my head itch, & ach, & burn like anything Mamma. This famous roll is not made *wholly* of a red *Cow Tail,* but is a mixture of that, & horsehair (very course) & a little human hair of yellow hue, that I suppose was taken out of the back part of an old wig . . . When it first came home, aunt put it on, & my new cap on it, she then took up her apron & mesur'd me, & from the roots of my hair on my forehead to the top of my notions, I mesur'd above an inch longer than I did downwards from the roots of my hair to the end of my chin.

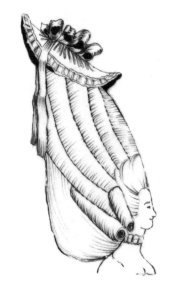

Nanny Green Winslow, age 11   Boston   1772 May 25

By the way, I was guilty of a sad mistake in London. I desired the servant to procure me a barber. The fellow stared, and was loth to ask for what purpose I wanted him. At last he said, "You mean a hair-dresser, Madam, I believe?" "Ay," says I, "I want my hair dressed." "Why, barbers, Madam, in this country, do nothing but shave."

Abigail Adams, age 40   Auteuil, France   1784 December 14

The fashionable shape of the ladies here is, to be very small at the bottom of the waist, and very large round the shoulders,—a wasp's,—pardon me, ladies, that I should make such a comparison, it is only in shape that I mean to resemble you to them. You and I, Madam, must despair of being in the mode.

Abigail Adams, age 40   Auteuil, France   1785 January 20

I have been in company with but one French Lady since I arrived ... This Lady I dined with at Dr Franklings [Benjamin Franklin] ... How said she I look? takeing hold of a dressing chemise made of tiffany which She had on over a blew Lutestring, and which looked as much upon the decay as her Beauty ... she had a small straw hat with a dirty half gauze hankerchief ... & a bit of dirtyer gauze than ever my maids wore was bowed on behind ... after dinner she threw herself upon a settee where she shew more than her feet. She had a little Lap Dog who was next to the Dr her favorite   this she kisst & when he wet the floor, she wiped it up with her chimise.

Abigail Adams, age 39   Auteuil, France   1784 September 5

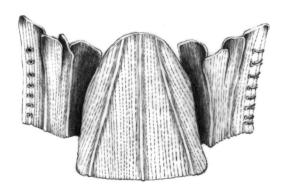

ABOVE

Eighteenth-century women wore corsets called stays, stiffened with strips of whalebone and laced at the back to lift the breasts and cinch the waist.

OPPOSITE

Towering hairdos were high fashion in the eighteenth century.
A paper of pins for use in sewing or for fastening gowns and kerchiefs at the bosom.

I was dress'd in my yellow coat, my black bib & apron, my pompedore shoes, the cap my aunt Storer sometime since presented me with (blue ribbins on it) & a very handsome loket in the shape of a hart she gave me—the past pin my Hond Papa presented me with in my cap, My new cloak & bonnet on, my pompedore gloves, &c. &c. And I would tell you, that *for the first time, they all lik'd my dress very much.*

Nanny Green Winslow, age 12   Boston   1772 January 4

The stile of dress which the preacher attacks is really an out-
rage upon all decency. I will describe it as it has appeard even
at the drawing Room—A sattin peticoat of certainly not more
than three breadths gored at the top, nothing beneath but a
chemise. Over this thin coat, a Muslin sometimes, sometimes
a crape made so strait before as perfectly to show the whole
form. The arm naked almost to the shoulder and without stays
or Bodice. A tight girdle round the waist, and the "rich Luxu-
rience of naturs Charms" without a hankerchief fully displayd.
The face, a la mode de Paris, Red as a Brick hearth. When
this Lady has been led up to make her curtzey, which she does
most gracefully, it is true, every Eye in the Room has been fixd
upon her, and you might litterally see through her. But in this
stile of dress, she has danced nor regarded the splitting out of
her scanty coat, upon the occasion. I asked a young Gentle-
man, if Miss.———was at the dance last Evening. The replie
was: yes, most wickedly.

Abigail Adams, age 55   Philadelphia   1800 March 18

Amongst the Ladies presented to me the Countess de Tilly
has been of the number . . . She has all the appearence and
dress of a Real French woman,   Rouged up to the Ears . . .

Abigail Adams, age 55   Philadelphia   1799 November 15

The observation did not in general hold good that fine feathers make fine birds—I saw many who were vastly richer drest than your Friends, but I will venture to say that I saw none neater or more elegant which praise I ascribe to the taste of mrs Temple & my mantua maker, for after having declared that I would not have any foil or tincel about me, they fix'd upon the dress I have described.

Abigail Adams, age 40   London   1785 June 24

I send you my dear Sister a piece of Muslin for two Crowns of caps. It must be done up with great care. It is calld Deca Muslin. It does not look well to tell the price of any thing which is for a present, but that you may know its real value, I will tell you that it was six dollors pr yd.

Abigail Adams, age 53   Philadelphia   1798 May 13

I am a little Surprized to find Dress unless upon publick occasions, so little regarded here, the gentlemen are very plainly Drest & the Ladies much less so than with us. Tis true you must put a hoop on & have your hair drest, but a common straw hat, no Cap, with only a ribbon upon the crown, is thought Dress sufficient to go into company.

Abigail Adams, age 39   London   1784 July 24

we *Diverted* Ourselves

In spite of their full schedules—and contrary to what most of us think—the scribblers did not work all the time, and they wrote often of their leisure-time activities. Their work itself brought respite. Many chores were seasonal, bringing the blessing of variety to everyday work. Certain work came, was accomplished, and was then ended for the year: apple harvesting, sheep shearing, whitewashing, and the like. Many of these major annual events were the occasion for work parties, when friends and neighbors gathered to join forces. Some ordinary everyday work, notably needlework, adapted itself to social visits—knitting and mending progressed unnoticed with talking. Quilting was customarily the occasion for a party. And one day out of seven, the scribblers laid aside all their work and devoted themselves to quiet meditation, or at least gave it a try.

The scribblers and their contemporaries worked steadily, to be sure; but they seemed to pace themselves and took pleasure when they could in visiting, reading, walking, sharing a cup of tea, or dancing, if they were young. They took notice of life's milestone events as opportunities for celebration and occasions for solemnity: weddings, birthdays, baptisms, funerals. They observed national holidays: Thanksgiving in fall, annual "fast days" in spring.

Like most American women, Nanny Green Winslow's circle enjoyed visiting and tea drinking on a regular basis. Nanny Green also wrote home about special events: regimental musters, Election Day, the "king's coronation day" in September (with fireworks), Valentine's Day, and the "annual Fast" in April. The highlight of Nanny Green's social life in Boston, however, was her own twelfth birthday, celebrated in fine style with eight young girlfriends, dancing, and refreshments. On another occasion she enjoyed a somewhat larger "constitution" or "assembly" with seventeen girls, two fiddlers, and minuets from five to ten o'clock.

Jemima Condict similarly noted Fast Day and Training Day, when men in the community practiced military drills and got together for a big meal. Jemima also enjoyed riding into Newark to shop, visits from friends, and occasionally attending parties or "frolicks."

Abby May, of all the scribblers, wrote the most about diversions because of her stay at a resort spa. Most of the guests were there for a vacation rather than because of serious illness, and the irony did not escape Abby. "It is and ever has been a strange circumstance to me that people should resort to a watering-place for pleasure," she observed wrily to Lucretia, "that they can dance and sing while disease and death continually stare them in the face." For entertainment, she and the others went for walks, drank tea, danced, and played games: billiards, checkers, "solitary" (played on the checker board), and "jingle the keys," a form of musical chairs. Some of the men gambled, to Abby's displeasure. Abby and her three beaux, Messrs. French, Townsend, and Brown, were fond of backgammon.

Abby enjoyed reading, writing, and music the most. A few of the guests sang, one played the flute, and once there was a concert with flute, violin, and "clarionet." On occasion small parties would go sightseeing. Abby visited a local iron refinery and pottery, went to see Indians who made and sold baskets, took day trips to Saratoga, and on one occasion went for several days to Lake George, where she went boating and toured historic Fort Ticonderoga with a guide.

In contrast, Aunt Bek Dickinson had little to say about diversions, which seem to have played little part in her life. She went to a wedding; there was a "great Training Day" in September 1789; she observed the public hanging of a young woman who had killed her own child. She went to church. Perhaps Bek's strict Calvinism had something to do with her relatively scanty observance of entertainment.

Leisure didn't seem to have much place in Molly Cooper's life, either, although her Long Island community offered a full measure of opportunity. She disapproved of dancing; her husband fretted over tea-drinking; there was a town meeting in April, "but no frolicing," to her satisfaction. The family was once invited to a "turtle feast," a sort of barbecue and a popular event in America at the time, but her husband wouldn't let them go (and her daughter Esther sulked all day). It comes as a surprise, then, to realize that Molly went on occasion to the horse races; not only that, she went on Sunday.

Another event Molly mentioned was barn-raising. The men joined forces to lift into place sections of the heavy timber frame (already hewn and jointed like pieces of a giant puzzle). The women worked together to prepare a meal of suitable proportions. There was often a dance afterward, to Molly's pique and Martha Ballard's pleasure. When the Ballards' sawmill burned down in 1788, a new frame went up shortly thereafter. Martha was thankful that only two men were hurt and that very few of the crowd were "disguised with Licquor." There was a dance for the "young folks," and everybody went home by midnight.

Like Molly, Martha also made note of "frolics" or "bees" based on textile work. Molly's girls went to sewing, spinning, and quilting frolics; Martha's daughters attended and hosted quilting parties. Martha regularly observed Fast Day in April and Thanksgiving. Neither Martha nor the other scribblers made much of Christmas. Protestant New England considered such practices too Papist and accordingly did without them, well into the nineteenth century.

Against this Yankee background of simple, utilitarian entertainment, the diversions Abigail Adams witnessed in Europe took on a rather sensational gleam. She observed—not with approval—that the French made pleasure "the business of life," and took a certain scandalized pleasure herself in describing favorite French pastimes: cards, whist, the opera, and, of course, *amour.* As Abigail noted, marriage French-style led in many homes to separate apartments for husband and wife and affairs that were scarcely concealed. When Abigail met Mme. de Lafayette, whom she admired, she reported that here was a wife "passionately attached to her Husband!!! a French Lady and fond of her Husband!!!" The dancers that Abigail saw at the Paris Opera disgusted her with their filmy outfits, but in spite of her disapproval she admitted to her sister that after the shock wore off she viewed the dances with pleasure. Abigail also went to see exhibitions of hot-air balloons, all the latest rage in France after the experiments of the Montgolfier brothers.

In London, Abigail continued her observations. The English were fond of the theater, she reported, and of gambling and seaside resorts. She visited Bath and Southampton, where she went bathing for the first time. Londoners supported a variety of entertainers: tumblers, tightrope dancers, and trained animals, including the famous "learned pig," dancing dogs, and a little hare that played the drums. "Dissipations," snorted Abigail, who preferred to stay at home with a good book.

The scribblers would be puzzled, I think, by our forty-hour work weeks and by some of our ideas of recreation. For them, work and leisure blended into an endless rhythm of activity from morning until night. Their choices for entertainment were fewer and their pleasures more often homemade.

Our treat was nuts, raisins, Cakes, Wine, punch, hot & cold, all in great plenty. We had a very agreeable evening from 5 to 10 o'clock. For variety we woo'd a widow, hunted the whistle, threaded the needle, & while the company was collecting, we diverted ourselves with playing of pawns, no rudeness Mamma I assure you.

Nanny Green Winslow, age 11   Boston   1772 January 17

I have never been in a situation in which morning noon & afternoon I have been half as much exposed to company ... I have returnd more than sixty visits all of them in 3 or 4 afternoons ...

Abigail Adams, age 44   Richmond Hill, New York   1789 August 9

My girls had some neighbours to help them quilt a bed quilt, 15 ladies. They began to quilt at 3h. p.m., finisht and took it out at 7, evening. There were 12 gentlemen took tea. They danced a little while after supper. Behaved exceeding cleverly. Were all returned home before the 11th h.

Martha Ballard, age 55   Augusta, Maine   1790 November 10

An eighteenth-century violin and wooden English transverse flute.

89

Tea Cakes.

*One pound sugar, half pound butter, two pound flour, three eggs,
one gill yeast, a little cinnamon and orange peel; bake fifteen minutes.*

Amelia Simmons, <u>American Cookery</u>

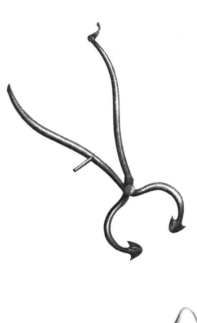

After Tea we four ramble'd into the woods, and found many
beauties—'tho I must confess Pine Trees and Musquitoes, were
more plenty than any other Commodity.

Abby May, age 24   Ballston Spa, New York   1800 June 9

You must know that there is a great Scarcity of Sugar and
Coffe, articles which the Female part of the State are very loth
to give up, especially whilst they consider the Scarcity occa-
siond by the merchants having secreted a large Quantity . . . It
was rumourd that an eminent, wealthy, stingy Merchant (who
is a Batchelor) had a Hogshead of Coffe in his Store which he
refused to sell to the committee under 6 shillings per pound.
A Number of Females some say a hundred, some say more
assembled with a cart and trucks, marchd down to the Ware
House and demanded the keys, which he refused to deliver,
upon which one of them seazd him by his Neck and tossed
him into the cart. Upon his finding no Quarter he deliverd the
keys, when they tipd up the cart and discharged him, then
opend the Warehouse, Hoisted out the Coffe themselves, put it
into the trucks and drove off.

    It was reported that he had a Spanking among them, but
this I believe was not true. A large concourse of Men stood
amazd silent Spectators of the whole transaction.

Abigail Adams, age 32   Braintree, Massachusetts   1777 July 31

We talk laugh drink
eat walk read play sing
every thing but work—
in short we are almost
hurried to death.

Abby May, age 24
Ballston Spa, New York
1800 July 8

Much company here.
Dade frets very much
caus they drinke tea.

Molly Cooper, age 55
Oyster Bay, Long Island
1769 May 25

It seams we have troublesome times a Coming for there is
great Disturbance a Broad in the earth & they say it is tea that
caused it. So then if they will Quarel about such a trifling
thing as that What must we expect But war & I think or at
least fear it will be so.

Jemima Condict, age 19   West Orange, New Jersey   1774 October 1

ABOVE
A silver coffeepot with wooden handle.

OPPOSITE
Iron nippers and a sugar loaf.

In the evening we had a smart ball . . . Doctr Anderson—
insisted upon my dancing . . . I found it did not fatigue me
and liking so good a medicine, I told the Dr. I should
take more of it than he directed.

Abby May, age 24   Ballston Spa, New York   1800 July 21

The first dance which I saw upon the stage shocked me. . . .
Girls cloathd in the thinnest silks & gauze, with their peticoats
short springing two foot from the floor poising themselves in
the air, with their feet flying and as perfectly shewing their
Garters & draws as tho no peticoat had been worn, was a
sight altogether new to me.

Abigail Adams, age 40   Auteuil, France   1785 February 20

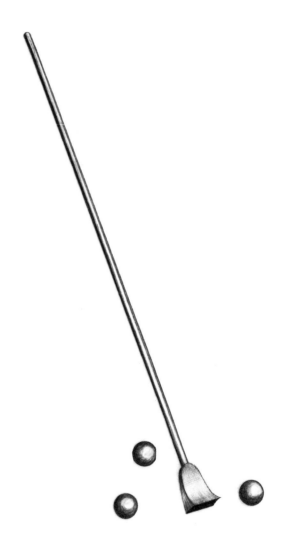

After dinner we all visited the Billiard room—some of the
ladies were said to play very well they certainly appear'd to
great advantage   tis a very graceful game—shows a fine
form—and hand and arm to the greatest advantage—rising
upon the toes the hand raised eyes fixed and the exercise
giving a fine glow to the cheeks—our ladies really look'd quite
killing. Our ladies knock'd about the Balls very adroitly,
and the homage of so many Beaux makes a game at
Billiards very fascinating.

Abby May, age 24   Ballston Spa, New York   1800

I went last week to hear the musick in Westminster Abbey.
The Messiah was performd. It was sublime beyond description
. . . I should have sometimes fancied myself amongst a higher
order of Beings; if it had not been for a very troublesome
female, who was unfortunately seated behind me; and whose
volubility not all the powers of Musick could still.

Abigail Adams, age 40   London   1785 June 6

ABOVE

A mahogany gaming table.

OPPOSITE

*Billiard balls and a cue
with a broad wooden tip.*

... I was at a stupid rout at the Swedish minister's last evening ... When a body has attended one of these parties, you know the whole of the entertainment. There were about two hundred persons present last evening. Three large rooms full of card-tables; the moment the ceremony of courtesying is past, the lady of the house asks you, "Pray, what is your game; whist, cribbage, or commerce?" ... I went with a determination not to play, but could not get off; so I was set down to a table with three perfect strangers, and the lady who was against me stated the game at half a guinea a-piece. I told her I thought it was full high; but I knew she designed to win, so I said no more, but expected to lose. It however happened otherwise. I won four games of her ... it was the luck of the cards rather than skill ... But such a set of gamblers as the ladies here are! and such a life as they lead! Good Heavens! were reasonable beings made for this?

Abigail Adams, age 41   London   1786 April 6

We made four couple at country dansing; danceing I mean.
In the evening young Mr. Waters hearing of my assembly, put
his flute in his pocket and played several minuets and other
tunes, to which we danced mighty cleverly.

Nanny Green Winslow, age 11   Boston   1771 November 30

... the ruins of fort Ticonderoga, and Lake Champlain
appear'd in view ... the ruins, much more magnificent then I
supposed existed in our new country, built of stone, and the
stone alone remaining ... we alighted, I paced over the stones
awestruck—this, said our guide was the house of the com-
manding officer ... Ah! thought I, how often has a proud step
and a gay heart passed thee, that now beats no more ... our
guide thought he knew a great deal, but I wish'd he knew
more ... of a spot that interested my feelings so much ... that
a vast sight of blood has been spilt on this spot, all agree—for
several miles round, every object confirms it—the heaps of
stones on which the soldiers used to cook—the ditches, now
grass grown, and forsaken graves!! all, every thing makes this
spot teem with melancholy reflections—

Abby May, age 24   Fort Ticonderoga, New York   1800 July 20

Canteburry is a larger town than Boston, it contains a number
of old Gothick Cathedrals, which are all of stone very heavy,
with but few windows which are grated with large Bars of
Iron, & look more like jails for criminals, than places designd
for the worship of the Deity, one would suppose from the
manner in which they are Guarded, that they apprehended
devotion would be stolen. They have a most gloomy appearance & realy made me shudder.

Abigail Adams, age 39   London   1784 July

One is obliged here to attend the circles of the Queen, which are held in summer once a fortnight, but once a week the rest of the year; and what renders it exceedingly expensive is, that you cannot go twice the same season in the same dress, and a Court dress you cannot make use of anywhere else ... We were placed in a circle round the drawing-room, which was very full, I believe two hundred persons present. Only think of the task! The royal family have to go round to every person, and find small talk enough to speak to all of them ... his Majesty saluted my left cheek; then asked me if I had taken a walk to-day. I could have told his Majesty that I had been all the morning preparing to wait upon him; but I replied, "No, Sire." "Why, don't you love walking?" says he ... The Queen was in purple and silver. She is not well shaped or handsome. As to the ladies of the Court, rank and title may compensate for want of personal charms; but they are, in general, very plain, ill-shaped, and ugly; but don't you tell anybody that I say so.

Abigail Adams, age 41   London   1786 June 26

I had envited some of my friends to come here to se Ester and dade would not let me have a turkey to rost for supper and I am so aflected   and ashamed about it that I feele as if I should never get over it.

Molly Cooper, age 56   Oyster Bay, Long Island   1771 February 2

ABOVE

Ladies of the English court as they were sometimes lampooned by political cartoonists.

OPPOSITE

A wooden doll with a painted face, c. 1790.

I drinked tea with brother and sister billing—with a great many fine Peopel who was a crouding in the ladies with there Silks   the men the happiest who could get the nearest to them.

Aunt Bek Dickinson, age 49   Hatfield, Massachusetts   1787 August 25

To-morrow is to be celebrated, *le jour des rois.* The day before this feast it is customary to make a large paste pie, into which one bean is put. Each person at table cuts his slice, and the one who is so lucky as to obtain the bean, is dubbed king or queen. Accordingly, to-day, when I went in to dinner, I found one upon our table.

Your cousin Abby began by taking the first slice; but alas! poor girl, no bean, and no queen. In the next place, your cousin John seconded her by taking a larger cut and . . . bisected his paste with mathematical circumspection; but to him it pertained not. By this time, I was ready for my part; but first I declared that I had no cravings for royalty. I accordingly separated my piece with much firmness, nowise disappointed that it fell not to me. Your uncle, who was all this time picking his chicken bone, saw us divert ourselves without saying any thing; but presently he seized the remaining half, and to crumbs went the poor paste, cut here and slash there; when, behold the bean! "And thus," said he, "are kingdoms obtained;" but the servant, who stood by and saw the havoc, declared solemnly that he could not retain the title, as the laws decreed it to chance, and not to force.

Abigail Adams, age 40   Auteuil, France   1785 January 24

Wee are envited
to a turtel feast
but Beene will not go
so we all staid at home.
Ester freted very greately.

Molly Cooper, age 55
Oyster Bay, Long Island
1769 September 11

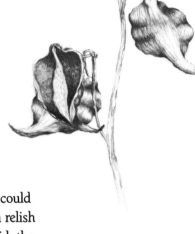

I believe this nation is the only one in the world which could make pleasure the business of life, and yet retain such a relish for it as never to complain of its being tasteless or insipid; the Parisians seem to have exhausted nature and art in this science, and to be "triste" is a complaint of a most serious nature.

Abigail Adams, age 39   Auteuil, France   1784 September 5

<u>Independence Cake</u>.

Twenty pound flour, 15 pound sugar, 10 pound butter, 4 dozen eggs, one quart wine, 1 quart brandy, 1 ounce nutmeg, cinnamon, cloves, mace, of each 3 ounces, two pound citron, currants and raisins 5 pound each, 1 quart yeast; when baked, frost with loaf sugar; dress with box and gold leaf.

Amelia Simmons, <u>American Cookery</u>

Ester and Becke
is hurreing away
to Hannah Yongs'
quilting frollic....

Molly Cooper, age 59
Oyster Bay, Long Island
1773 September 9

To day will be the 5th great dinner I have had, about 36 Gentlemen to day, as many more next week, and I shall have got through the whole of Congress, with their apendages. Then comes the 4 July which is a still more tedious day, as we must then have not only all Congress, but all the Gentlemen of the city, the Governour and officers and companies, all of whom the late President used to treat with cake, punch and wine . . . As we are here we cannot avoid the trouble nor the expence. I have been informd the day used to cost the late President 500 dollors. More than 200 wt of cake used to be expended, and 2 quarter casks of wine besides spirit. You will not wonder that I dread it, or think President Washington to blame for introducing the custom, if he could have avoided it.

Abigail Adams, age 52   Philadelphia   1797 June 23

Bittersweet (above)
and milkweed (opposite).

We are busie cooking for the work men. Evening, they eate ther supper. The more parte went away. Some stay to dance, very greately against my will.

Molly Cooper, age 55   Oyster Bay, Long Island   1769 September 30

Friday July 4th Independance—but sadly, shamefully neglected
... every one felt as if it was a great Day, but no preparations
were made to keep it, and the hours wore away in languor
and fatigue—a Ball was in contemplation, but no music could
be procur'd. I threaten'd to set fire to the bathing house, by
way of amusement.

Abby May, age 24   Ballston Spa, New York   1800 July 4

Mrs Farmer ... asked me to take a syllabub with her in the
evening ... in the midst of wild bushes and tall pines, was
erected a delightful arbour, or bowry—20 feet square—open
at the sides, but the top covered with green boughs, and the
hemlock hung over the sides like a fringe—the four posts
which supported the roof were bound round with green—and
red and white holly oak—pots of flowers were distributed—
and benches placed round the sides—in the centre was a
table handsomly covered with, syllabub, cream, raspberries,
currants, cakes, rusk, &cc. a cooler, contain'd liquor for the
gentlemen—the effect was delightful.

Abby May, age 24   Ballston Spa, New York   1800 July 12

To make a fine Syllabub from the Cow.

*Sweeten a quart of cyder with double refined sugar, grate nutmeg
into it, then milk your cow into your liquor, when you have thus
added what quantity of milk you think proper, pour half a pint or
more, in proportion to the quantity of syllabub you make, of the
sweetest cream you can get all over it.*

Amelia Simmons, American Cookery

I Went to Newark I and my Sisters. We thought to Have had
A good Deal of pleasure that Day But Before I got Home I
had a like to have Had my Neck broke   I rid a young Horse
and it Was a very windy day and the Dirt flew and there Was
chairs and Waggons a rattling and it scared the horse so that
he started and flung me of and sprained my arm . . .

Jemima Condict, age 17   West Orange, New Jersey   1772 June 10

New Year's Cake.

*Take 14 pound flour, to which add one pint milk, and one quart
yeast, put these together over night, and let it lie in the sponge till
morning, 5 pound sugar and 4 pound butter, dissolve these
together, 6 eggs well beat, and carroway seed; put the whole
together, and when light bake them in cakes, similar to breakfast
biscuit, 20 minutes.*

Amelia Simmons, American Cookery

There is a kind of cake in fashion upon this day call'd New
Years Cooky. This & Cherry Bounce as it is calld is the old
Dutch custom of treating their Friends upon the return of
every New Year. The common people, who are very ready to
abuse Liberty, on this day are apt to take rather too freely of
the good things of this Life, and finding two of my servants
not all together qualified for Business, I remonstrated to them,
but they excused it by saying it was New Year, & every body
was joyous then.

Abigail Adams, age 45   Richmond Hill, New York   1790 January 5

O WHAT A *Fine Thing* IS HEALTH!

Health was a topic of prime concern to the scribblers. They were interested in their own well-being, of course, and deeply concerned with the well-being of their families and friends. As women they were responsible for general health care at home. Diagnosing, dispensing remedies, and around-the-clock nursing or "watching" were all part of traditional housewifery. Their diaries and letters give a detailed account of their ailments and treatments, and distinctive ways in which each coped with illness.

From what she wrote, Nanny Green Winslow was evidently a sound little soul who only occasionally had minor troubles with sore eyes or a cold. Her most serious complaint was an outbreak of boils on her hips and hands, which her aunt doctored at home with poultices, plasters, and a half-ounce dose of "globe Salt," or Glauber's salt, a popular cathartic and a "disagreeable potion." Through it all, Nanny Green kept her usual sense of humor. When she broke out anew with boils, Nanny Green wrote home that she was to undergo "another seasoning" with the salt.

Jemima Condict likewise enjoyed relatively good health, or at least met her ailments with fortitude. Like most of her contemporaries, Jemima occasionally suffered from toothache; she wrote in detail of the usual treatment, extraction by a local doctor. Dental anesthesia was unknown. Other scribblers as well wrote of tooth-pulling as a common event.

Though Jemima was fortunate to escape serious illness in a wave of epidemics that swept her community, her diary makes clear that no one really escaped the onslaught of "sickly times." Those who were spared illness themselves faced the loss of family and friends and suffered the anxiety of not knowing who might next be struck. Jemima and others watched and waited with dread as smallpox, "sorethroat distemper," and the "bloody flux" (a severe bowel disorder) claimed their victims. In most cases, preventive measures beyond prayer were unknown.

Smallpox was an exception. Although inoculation was a relatively new and potentially hazardous procedure in its own right, a growing number of people chose the risks of a mild case under controlled circumstances to avoid the possibility of contracting this debilitating and disfiguring disease in its full force. Both Jemima and Molly Cooper mentioned friends who were inoculated, though both feared the outcome. Abby May's little brother George was inoculated en route to Ballston Spa when Mrs. May learned of smallpox in nearby Albany. Before their marriage, John Adams underwent inoculation in Boston, describing the unpleasant procedure to Abigail in letters which were carefully smoked to prevent the spread of infection. Later, Abigail had her small children inoculated when smallpox broke out in Boston.

As an invalid, Abby May understandably devoted much of her attention to medical matters during her stay at the health spa. We don't really know what was the matter with Abby's hand, the cause of her suffering. Neither did her doctors, whose efforts to relieve her of the painful spasms included opium, a common prescription that had at least the benefit of pain-killing. The fashionable water cure was Abby's reason for visiting Ballston Spa during the summer of 1800. Like other ailing hopefuls, Abby "took the waters" in all possible ways— bathing in the springs three days a week, drinking two quarts of the mineral water each day, and four times daily having her flannel-wrapped hand doused with the water and massaged.

Though her mysterious ailment caused her pain and frustration, Abby tried hard to maintain her spirits. On occasion she distracted herself and Lucretia with accounts of the other guests and their complaints. One woman had an "ulcer opened"; others suffered with "inverted Gout," rheumatism, salt rheum (a skin disease like eczema), and scrofula, which caused swelling of the lymph glands.

To cure a headache, her mother drank bitter wormwood tea; if it worsened, she tried poultices and laudanum, a form of opium, which left her "heavy and low spirited." A woman severely bruised in a wagon accident was "blooded" by the doctor, a ubiquitous treatment. Abby felt particular sympathy for a little girl badly burned when her muslin slip caught fire, and for an unfortunate child "continually on the twitch" with a disorder called St. Anthony's fire, an infection of the skin similar to erypsipelas. Abby's accounts also underscore the problem that modesty caused for women and their male doctors. When she had "a little of the Dysentary," or diarrhea, Abby could not bring herself to mention the problem to her doctor, but relied on a female friend to administer powders of rhubarb and "Epecac."

Physically, Aunt Bek Dickinson was a tough old bird. The only illness she mentioned was "the collick," which she got every September and for which she was bled by the local doctor. Bek's most serious ailment was caused by an accident. When a bad windstorm blew the roof off her house, burying Bek in the rubble, she managed to crawl out, called a doctor, who bled her some more, and recovered after three days in bed. Sounder in body than Abby May, Bek shared Abby's struggles with melancholy. "This day I am not Composed," she wrote one day, "my mind is like a kite in the air." On other days she came home and cried alone in her empty house, then berated herself for not accepting God's will.

Of all the scribblers, it was Molly Cooper who complained most about feeling unwell. "I am unwell and sore distrest," Molly wrote in many entries. Occasionally she specified a cause: the "cholic," a nosebleed, pain in her back and hip, a fall from her horse, "a mighty cold in my heade so that I can very hardly breeth." Molly also worried about her family's health. "Dade," her husband, had ague fits, sometimes so severe that the doctor had to come. Esther, her daughter, nearly died with the colic. Smallpox terrified Molly, who watched fearfully as some of her circle went to the "pox house" for inoculation and quarantine. Hand in hand with Molly's poor physical condition went her emotional state. Fatigue and darkness seemed always to be with her.

In contrast, Abigail Adams met infirmity head on. "A merry heart does good like a medicine," she was fond of quoting from Proverbs, and with characteristic fortitude she weathered suffering as it came. As a young wife and mother she survived an epidemic of dysentery that swept through Braintree and left her mother among the dead.

In spite of good physical health, however, even Abigail's "merry heart" was sorely tried by John's long silences during his absences. The letters Abigail wrote in her late thirties reveal bouts of acute depression. "Alass my dear I am much afflicted with a disorder call'd the

Heartach," she wrote in 1781 when she had not heard from him in fifteen months, "nor can any remedy be found in America . . ."

In later life in Philadelphia, Abigail nursed her teenage son Tommy through a severe illness (probably rheumatic fever) with the help of Dr. Benjamin Rush, one of the country's foremost physicians. The doctor also looked into her "inflamitory Rhumatism," a chronic complaint. "Dr. Rush is for calling it Gout, but I will not believe a word of all that, for Rhumatism I have had ever since I was a child," decided Abigail, who persisted in treating herself with a home-made concoction of powdered nitre (used also in gunpowder and as a meat preservative), tartar emetic (a poisonous salt also used in dyeing cloth), and calomel, a common purgative. Abigail came down with a bad fever in Philadelphia, which may have been malaria, but escaped the deadly yellow fever epidemic that killed an estimated one in ten in that area in the 1790s.

Of all the scribblers, Martha Ballard wrote far and away the most about health matters. As a professional midwife and nurse, she used her journals as a record of her experience, incidentally leaving a goldmine of specific information on late eighteenth-century medical practice. Martha's career in medicine began formally in 1778, at age forty-three, when she started working as an assistant to an established midwife. Her training was on-the-job and in the nature of an apprenticeship. Much of her know-how was based on an ancient body of medicinal folklore; the rest was unquestionably trial and error.

Martha's journals reveal to how great an extent community health care was in the hands of women. There were at least three male doctors in Martha's locale, but their presence seems to have been requested only in extreme circumstances. Martha evidently coexisted harmoniously with them, occasionally buying supplies from them and once attending a "Decexion," or autopsy, with twelve physicians and two other midwives. As a general practictioner, Martha handled a wide range of cases. Over the years Martha treated burns, sore backs, sprains, frostbite, cuts, and accidental poisonings; coughs, sore throats, colds, fevers, earaches, headaches, and asthma; worms, shingles, rashes, dropsy, colic, apoplexy, and "shocks of the palsy," or strokes; and chicken pox, whooping cough, "St. Vites Daunce," and mumps.

Martha also served as pharmacist to the community. In contrast to the doctors, who relied heavily on bleeding and commercially available drugs, Martha treated her patients mostly with homemade remedies. Poultices, plasters, blisters, salves, and "decoctions," or teas, were her stock-in-trade. A list of her ingredients sounds like a grocery list: salt and pepper, beeswax, honey, eggs, vinegar, flour, nutmeg, red pepper, rhubarb, hops, currants, and licorice were some of the items she used. Many of Martha's remedies involved herbs: feverfew, tansy, sage, camomile, lavender, wormwood, pennyroyal, hyssop, rue, mugwort, burdock, mullein, sorrel, and gold thread were in her pharmacopoeia. Martha also made use of standard prepared medicinal substances: jalap and calomel, both purgative powders; senna and manna, imported laxatives; dragon's blood, from palm trees; castor oil; spirit, or rubbing alcohol; vitriol, or sulfuric acid; and nitre. Strong-smelling camphor was an all-round remedy, as was rum (used externally, as, for example, in a burn salve made of equal parts rum, onions, and cornmeal).

Martha's experience as a midwife makes her journals exceptionally valuable for their insight into childbirth practices and other health concerns specific to women. Like other women in eighteenth-century America, Martha and her patients considered childbirth as women's business. Male physicians were called only in cases of extreme danger. Normally, women gave birth at home attended by a midwife and in the comforting presence of close female friends and family. In her career, Martha delivered 996 babies. Contrary to what we often assume about the hazards of infant mortality, the vast majority of Martha's deliveries were successful, although many were difficult. For her service, Martha charged eight shillings but often took her fee in trade. Rum, sugar, coffee, salt, flatirons, shoes, butter, wheat, rye, calico, linen, and rice were some of the goods Martha accepted as payment.

If there is a common thread in the scribblers' accounts of sickness and health, it is a sense of inescapable mortality. Death struck swiftly and often. The marking of birthdays was an occasion for gratitude for another year past and speculation if another birthday would safely follow.

Loss of children was the rule, not the exception, and a circumstance with which the scribblers were sorrowfully acquainted. Two of Nanny Green Winslow's brothers died young. Martha Ballard lost three daughters, aged two, four, and eight, within two weeks when she was thirty-four, and just a month before giving birth to another daughter, Hannah. Abigail Adams lost Susanna, her one-year-old, and later mourned the birth of a stillborn daughter. Abigail lived to see her son Charlie die as a young man and her daughter Nabby succumb at age forty-nine to breast cancer following what was without question a dreadful operation. Saddest of all, Molly Cooper outlived all six of her children.

And yet, a sense of acceptance comes through in the scribblers' words as well. Sickness and death were part of their lives, matters of faith, beyond human control. If the available medical care was inadequate according to our standards, they at least had the comfort of dying at home in the care of those they loved best.

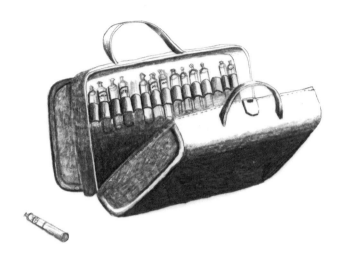

Went to See my
Cousin J. W. She being
not well & I Dont think
ever will Be. O What
a fine thing is health!

Jemima Condict, age 19
West Orange, New Jersey
1774 October 14

Six months have Passed over my head . . . what a scene of
health and Prosperity has Passed over my head   Sickness that
distressing trouble has not Come nigh me my days have
Passed in health and Plenty the Spring Creeps on beautifully.

Aunt Bek Dickinson, age 56   Hatfield, Massachusetts   1795 April 5

Doctr Anderson thinks he can cure me—if the waters fail—
Mr. Dobson thinks Animal Magnetism will, Mr. Hubbard is
persuaded, Dr Porter of Connecticut will relieve me, if I will
go to Newhaven—and Dr Kittredge of Pittsfield, is certain he
could restore me, and my hand, to perfect health—if all these
fail—Why by that time something else will be started.

Abby May, age 24   Ballston Spa, New York   1800 June 17

A doctor's bag
with vials of medicines.

Mrs. Heartwell here for herbs; one of her children is unwell. Capt. Purington's little sons for same, for their marm, she being unwell.

Martha Ballard, age 70   Augusta, Maine   1806 February 18

I am unwell and much aflected for fear of the small pox. . . . I got to bed feard and distressed at 1 or 2 o'clock in the morning.

Molly Cooper, age 56   Oyster Bay, Long Island   1771 February 2

I have a Lad who has been sick a week, and that from eating Ice creeme when he was making it & hot. He brought on such a cramp in His stomack that his Life has been in danger ever since.

Abigail Adams, age 52   Philadelphia   1797 June 8

Tis a fortnight to Night since I wrote you a line during which, I have been confined with the Jaundice, Rhumatism and a most voilent cold; I yesterday took a puke which has relieved me, and I feel much better to day.

Abigail Adams, age 31   Weymouth, Massachusetts   1775 November 27

Every body says that this is a bitter cold day, but I know nothing about it but hearsay for I am in aunt's chamber (which is very warm always) with a nice fire, a stove, sitting in Aunt's easy chair, with a tall three leav'd screen at my back, & I am very comfortable.

Nanny Green Winslow, age 11   Boston   1772 February 13

Mrs. Nason called in to get some dock root for the itch.

*Martha Ballard, age 71
Augusta, Maine
1807 May 5*

It is most terible cold
& I am aforst to be in the Shop
for I have to weave. I cant
get a long with it.

Jemima Condict, age 24
West Orange, New Jersey
1779 December

My fingers are so cold
I can scarcely hold a pen.

Abigail Adams, age 44
Braintree, Massachusetts
1788 December 18

ABOVE

Tansy, a traditional remedy
for "female complaints."

OPPOSITE

Mullein, good for chest
and lung ailments as well
as for repelling fleas.

Resolved if Possible to have my toth out So Down I went to Dr. C. and he got his Cold iron ready ... I new hed hurt but I Could Not make him Promis he would Not; tho I thought he began to Pety me a Little & that was what I Did it for; for its true I believe I want so fraid as I pretended to be. I was In hopes he'd Draw it easer for it & I Dont know but he Did for he was mighty Carefull, but when he Put his Contrivance in my mouth I puld them out agin. At Last they fell a lafing at me & Said if I dast not have A tooth Drawd I Never would be fit to marry. I told them I never Recond to be if twas as Bad as to have a toth Drawd. At which they all fell a lauging for I was fooll for them; but it want Long before I could put my Toth in my pocket & laugh with the Best of them.

Jemima Condict, age 20   West Orange, New Jersey   1775

I fear Mr. Cranch does not put on his flannel soon enough. I grow more and more in favour of the use of it and advise you to wear it next your skin. Make little waistcoats & put them on with the first comeing of cold weather, & [if] I had as much spair Room in my stays as you have I would not be without them.

Abigail Adams, age 45   New York   1790 October 10

Come to this house about half after seven and found it dark and lonesome here. I walked the rooms and cryd myself sick and found my heart very stubborn against the government of God who has set me here for to try my fidelity to my lord who knows the best way.

Aunt Bek Dickinson, age 49   Hatfield, Massachusetts   1787 September 2

Doctr Stringer thinks highly of the Oxygen Gas—and would wish to try it in my case but not yet—he advises me to use opium, I asked him why . . . and also asked if it possessed active medical virtue equal to removing a complaint, as I supposed it only capable of lulling for a time not radically curing any disorder . . . From his reply I found opium was the word with him, however, tis better than poultices and vitae—besides the prescribers venerable & scientific appearance and conversation, reconciled me to his prescription more than if it had been made by a quacking ragamuffin—such is the force of prejudice.

The opium has a worse effect than yesterday. When I had about half done breakfast I felt very odly and rose from table. I know no more till half past eleven. But Mrs Lowell says I told all my secrets, and talked incessantly . . . and was very amusing. The Doct'r call'd and said I had taken too large a dose, but ought not to be discouraged, and he divided all the pills into quarters.

Abby May, age 24   Ballston Spa, New York   1800

A fine clear morning.
The early songsters warbling
thier notes and all nature seemes
to smile, but a darke cloud
hangs continuly over my soul
and makes the days and nights
pass heavily along.

Molly Cooper, age 54
Oyster Bay, Long Island
1769 May 3

Tis said of Cato the roman censor, that one of the 3 things which he regreted during his Life, was going once by sea when he might have made his journey by land; I fancy the philosopher was not proof against that most disheartning, disspiriting malady—Sea Sickness . . . I have had frequent occasion Since I came on Board, to recollect an observation of my best Friends, " that no Being in Nature was so disagreeable as a Lady at Sea."

Abigail Adams, age 39   Aboard ship on the Atlantic   1784 July 6

The doctor is gone
thow mercy.

Molly Cooper, age 54
Oyster Bay, Long Island
1769 February 10

3 Times was I let Blood,
the state of which was like
a person in a high plurisy.
I am now lame in my wrists
from the 8th pr of Blisters
which I have had.

Abigail Adams, age 47
Braintree, Massachusetts
1792 March 20

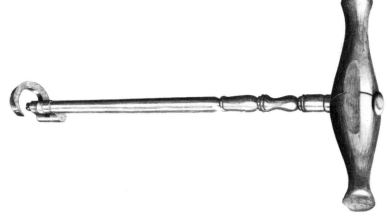

Bless me! what a catalogue of human infirmities might be pub-lish'd from these Springs—I am told their is very few here now—Yet there is the nervous, Rheumatic, Spasmatic, Crazatic, Itchatic, Hypiatic, Goutatic, Soreatic, and all the atics—beside scorbutic, scrophulous and headachs.

Abby May, age 24   Ballston Spa, New York   1800 June 7

At the Congress spring I was really pleased beyond my expec-tations ... I was so well satisfied with the flavour of the wa-ters—I drank four large half pints ... When we leave here, I know not what we shall do for a substitute—and have not made up my mind wether toddy or gin sling will do best—being used to water of so high a flavour—Adams Ale, is so insipid I can scarcely wash my mouth with it.

Abby May, age 24   Saratoga, New York   1800 June 20

A blood letter
and a tooth extractor.

... I will see that the Baby shall have every necessary article. I shall be answerable to the Nurse for its Board, but they made the poor thing sick by taking it out in the Evening and giving it Rum, the Nurse says to make it sleep.

Abigail Adams, age 53   Philadelphia   1789 April 22

I am very well
& sleep soundly—
when I am not vexed.

Abigail Adams, age 55
Philadelphia
1800 April 15

Join with me my dearest Friend in Gratitude to Heaven, that a life I know you value, has been spaired and carried thro Distress and danger altho the dear Infant is numberd with its ancestors ... it appeard to be a very fine Babe, and as it never opened its Eyes in this world it lookd as tho they were only closed for sleep ... My Heart was much set upon a Daughter.

Abigail Adams, age 32   Braintree, Massachusetts   1777 July 16

This morning here alone
like a Sparrow alone
on the hous top my
Sollatary hours are many.

Aunt Bek Dickinson, age 49
Hatfield, Massachusetts
1787 September 13

William McMaster expired at 3 o'clock. Mrs. Paten and I laid out the child. Poor mother! how distrest her case; near the hour of labour and those children never very sick! Now at home; it is nine o'clock, morn. I feel depres't. I must take some rest.

Martha Ballard, age 52   Augusta, Maine   1787 August 13

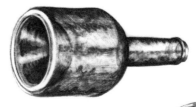

I was at Wm. Chamberlain's. My patient is not very well. We find she has an inclination to drink rhum. She drank about 1 quart.

Martha Ballard, age 61   Augusta, Maine   1796 April 6

Children, I have been called to the birth of this year past, 28, — seventeen of them were daughters. I have lost 42 nights' sleep this year past.

Martha Ballard, age 50   Augusta, Maine   1785 December 31

I cannot find a cook
in the whole city but what
will get drunk . . .

Abigail Adams, age 44
Richmond Hill, New York
1789 August 9

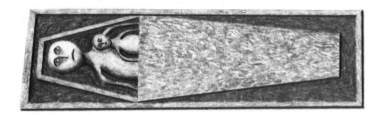

I heard . . . that Mrs. Claton's child departed this life yesterday, and that she was thot expiring. . . . She departed this life about 1 p.m. I asisted to lay her out; her infant laid in her arms, the first such instance I ever saw, and the first woman that died in childbed which I delivered.

Martha Ballard, age 52   Augusta, Maine   1787 August 20

The Lord Was pleased To Remove by Death my Cousin Jotham Cundict. He Was aged 19 years And one month lord grant that this stroke of thy providence May be for my good. O that it might awaken me o that it might take a right efect upon me.

Jemima Condict, age 17   West Orange, New Jersey   1772 April 25

Our House has been a mere Hospital ever since Saturday last.
I have been confined in one chamber, Col. Smith in an other
with a Billious attack, Charles in an other with a fever, my
Housekeeper confind to her chamber with Saint Antonys fire,
and a servant of Col. Smiths laid up with a voilent seazure of
the Breast & Lungs, but thanks to a kind Providence we are all
upon the Recovery.

Abigail Adams, age 45   Richmond Hill, New York   1790 April 28

Was took With The measels and on Monday Night I Broke
out in My face and Hand. on Tuesday I was as Red as a
Chery And I Was of a fine Coular. My measels Turnd on
Wednesday But still felt very Mean all that week and a Sunday.
yet is Great Mercy Shown to me I want so bad As Some.

Jemima Condict, age 16   West Orange, New Jersey   1772 August 16

Merial Heartwell here
for my pan to warm
her marm's bed;
says she is very unwell.

Martha Ballard, age 70
Augusta, Maine
1806 February 19

Was my Cousins Knockulated   I am apt to think they will
repent there Undertaking before they Done with it for I
am Shure tis a great venter. But Sence they are gone I wish
them Sucses And I think they have Had good luck So far for
they have all Got home Alive . . .

Jemima Condict, age 19   West Orange, New Jersey   1775 February 5

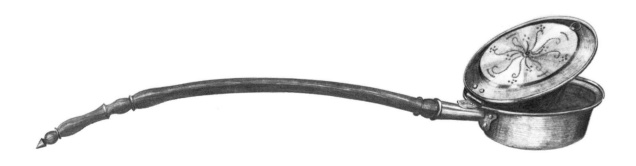

I felt most wretchedly
but went to clearstarching muslins
to drive away fatigue.

Abby May, age 20
Portland, Maine
1796 August

Clear. I have done a large
washing for me, since 12 o'clock,
and washt my kitchen. Thus I
end this year. It is of God's
mercy that I am yet alive and
able to perform my business.

Martha Ballard, age 70
Augusta, Maine
1805 December 31

This is the anniversary of my birth; 73 years have I seen; past
thro many sceins. May it please the Great Parent of the universe to enable me to live devoted to his service the little time
I have to sojourn in this world.

Martha Ballard, age 73   Augusta, Maine   1808 February 20

Mr. Ballard is very sick yet. My hopes almost vanisht that he
will recover, but God is infinitely good and wise in all his
dealings with us, and I really wish to be able to say, his will be
done!!! but how hard it is thus to say. . . .

Martha Ballard, age 63   Augusta, Maine   1799 September 10

Martha Ballard

FIXED A REMEDY

Mrs. Dexter very ill
with the mumps;
fixed her a remedy
and she mended soon.

Martha Ballard, age 50
Augusta, Maine
1785 September 26

Mr. Davis came here,
he has the shingles.
We bled a cat and
applied the blood
which gave him relief.

1786 October 13

At my son's;
his little son
burnt his head,
we applied
rhum and salt.

1793 January 30

I was called in great
haste to see Mrs. Ham-
len who was in a fitt . . .
Applyed vinagar to
her lips, temples, and
hands, and onions
to her feet, and
shee revived.

1790 October 14

I was called out of
bed this morn to go
and see Mrs. Waid
who has the collic.
I gave her some red
pepper, steept, and
she got ease soon,
and was able to
sett up and work,
afternoon.

1796 May 30

I find Patty very sick.
I put black wool wet
with brandy and pepper
into her ears, which gave
her present relief.

1798 December 6

O, I am sik all day long.
Up very late but I have got
my cloths iorned.

Molly Cooper, age 54
Oyster Bay, Long Island
1769 April 22

We here Alsop's child is very sik. Oh Lord, have mercy on that famaly. Spare the children, O Lord, and bless the young woman and all thos conserned with the saveing helth of thy salvation. O, let them live and not dy.

Molly Cooper, age 56   Oyster Bay, Long Island   1771 March 19

This Day I am eighteen year old the Lord has been So Mercyfull to me as to spare me so long . . .

Jemima Condict, age 18   West Orange, New Jersey   1772 August 24

Presented with the happy prospect that my dear companion is some better. . . . Great God the glory shall be thine.

Martha Ballard, age 63   Augusta, Maine   1799 September 11

This day is eleven years since my dear son Isaac departed this life. Sorrow, sorrow and loss unspakabel.

A mortar and pestle, a sieve,
and a chopper and bowl.

Molly Cooper, age 56   Oyster Bay, Long Island   1771 May 8

Knowledge IS A FINE THING

In the scribblers' world, education was not something to take for granted. School systems were haphazard at best and had not been helped by the disruptions of the war. Universal free public education was long in the future.

In the absence of reliable schools, families interested in education had several options, all of which cost something. They could send their children to private schools as day or boarding students, hire tutors, or place the children with neighborhood women who operated informal schools out of their homes. Other families might instruct their own children at home or simply forgo the whole business. In light of the situation, it was not surprising that many Americans could neither read nor write. Though desirable, formal education was, after all, not indispensable.

Schooling for girls was especially questionable. While there was no question that abilities to read, write, and do simple arithmetic were important for reading the Bible and keeping household accounts, further training seemed unnecessary. History, geography, French, literature, and other academic subjects were not likely to be of use in most women's adult lives.

As a result, education for women veered in two sharply diverging directions. For most girls it meant practical instruction in domestic work and possibly specialized training as an apprentice in cookery, plain sewing, or other female trades. For upper-class girls, there were finishing schools with lessons in etiquette, fancy needlework, dancing, music, fine penmanship, and other accomplishments expected of a lady. For all, the single most influential teacher was the church, where weekly instruction in moral education continued throughout a woman's life.

Where did the scribblers fit? The mere fact of their literacy distinguished them from most of their contemporaries. They not only knew how to write; they chose to write above and beyond the necessities of household routine. Each had obviously received some schooling. Their diaries and letters reveal some of the ways that thinking women felt about learning, books, religion, and the place of educated women in the world beyond the household.

For some of the scribblers, education was not a primary concern. Jemima Condict, Aunt Bek Dickinson, and Molly Cooper had little to say about schools or books. The church, however, played a major role in the lives of each.

Jemima Condict devoted a large part of her journal to recording the weekly text in morning and afternoon sermons at the Mountain Society Presbyterian Church. Jemima took religion seriously and was troubled by the state of her soul. Sorrow for her "Sins without Number" and dissatisfaction with herself were a frequent theme. "I spent this evening in Writeing But the worst of it is what I write is Noncense," she chided herself in 1774. "If I Did But Write that would Be instructive or that would Do me any good or any one else twould be some Sence in Spending Time & Paper. But No wonder I Can write Nothing thats good for I Dont Do anything thats good." Apart from sermons, Jemima's education was scanty. It seems likely that her formal schooling was limited to a session in childhood with "Mrs. D.W." If Jemima read books, she didn't mention them in her journal. Her grammar and spelling were not polished.

Aunt Bek Dickinson's writing was similarly untutored. At one point in her life she nearly threw out her journals—"they are wrote and Spelt So Poorly that it works me to See them," she grumbled. Like Jemima, Bek used her journal to make note of the sermons she heard. The Reverend Mr. Lyman pleased her; after seventeen years, she found him still "as Strict a Calvinist as I could wish."

Molly Cooper was even more intensely involved with the church. The conversion of Molly at age fifty-five from the established Anglican church to the New Light Baptists in 1769 precipitated a flood of religious commentary in her diary. Worship meetings—including covenant meetings on Saturdays and several meetings throughout the day on Sundays—were an important part of Molly's life. When weather or visitors kept her from attending, Molly felt grievous indeed. Her husband Joseph, a Quaker, did not share in Molly's zeal. We don't know what education beyond church Molly had; nor did she mention books or school for her children. Her writing was perhaps the poorest of the seven scribblers.

The other four scribblers showed more interest in reading and education—a fact reflected both in their orthography and in their subject matter.

Nanny Green Winslow was at school when she wrote her journal, which in fact was part of her homework, a way of practicing her composition and penmanship. Her accounts give a glimpse of the experience of an unusually privileged girl sent to private schools in Boston. Although Nanny Green wrote more about her home life and fashions than about her lessons, we know that she went to a writing school where Master Samuel Holbrook was her instructor, and to a sewing school operated by Madam Smith.

Books were part of Nanny Green's life, and she was evidently an avid reader. From her cousin Charles she borrowed "The puzzeling cap," a riddle book, and the "history of Gaffer too-shoes," probably the story of the character better known as Little Goody Two-shoes. Charles also lent her *Gulliver's Travels* in an abridged version, which her aunt encouraged her to read. Jonathan Swift, the Irish author, had died only fifteen years before Nanny Green was born; the famous satire had been in print for almost fifty years.

Nanny was also among the first ranks of novel readers—the genre had been introduced only some thirty years earlier by Samuel Richardson. Since books tended to appear and circulate much more slowly in Nanny Green's day than in our own, novels remained widely read for decades. The popular *Sir Charles Grandison* by Richardson, which Nanny Green read in 1772, had first appeared several decades earlier. On New Year's Day in 1772 Nanny Green was delighted to recieve an "abreviated" children's edition of *Joseph Andrews*, handsomely bound "In nice Guilt" and with flowered covers. This, the first novel of Henry Fielding, the author of *Tom Jones*, had been in print for thirty years. Nanny Green also read stories in *The Mother's Gift*, a collection of moral tales "for all little children who wish to be good." Of course, she read the Bible regularly.

Abby May was even more of a bookworm and keenly felt the lack of books at the spa hotel, which she ransacked for reading matter. She did fairly well. During the summer of 1800 she managed to find at least three novels only thirty to fifty years old: *Tristram Shandy*, a wildly unconventional and somewhat scandalous novel by Laurence Sterne; *The Vicar of Wakefield* by Oliver Goldsmith, who died the year before Abby was born; and *Peregrine Pickle* by Tobias Smollett, a comic adventure story.

Abby also dipped into poetry (sonnets by Charlotte Smith, a contemporary English romantic novelist); drama (by the German playwright Friedrich Schiller, then barely in his forties); and philosophy (an aesthetics treatise on the "Sublime and Beautiful" by Edmund Burke, better known as a political theorist). For older classics Abby turned to *Paradise Lost* by Milton and the clever maxims of La Rochefoucauld, both from the century before. For periodicals there was a stray issue of *The Connoisseur.*

Although Abby didn't discuss her schooling, her journal and her sophistication were clearly the products of a fine education. Abby sprinkled her pages with quotes from Lord Chesterfield, noted for his urbanity and polished wit. It seems evident that Abby's upbringing placed as much emphasis on development of the intellect as it did on that of the soul.

We don't know what Martha Ballard experienced in the way of formal education, but she showed interest in basic schooling for her children and grandchildren. At age twelve her son Ephraim went to school; the girls attended singing school. In 1804 Martha noted the raising of a schoolhouse with civic pride. The next year, several of her grown children went to school and her grandson Jack was sent to grammar school. Martha's tastes in reading were practical: though she didn't seem to have time for books, she did try to keep up with the newspapers that came on an irregular basis.

Of all the scribblers, Abigail Adams held education in the highest regard. Ironically, Abigail herself never had a formal education. Childhood health problems forced her to stay at home, where lessons from her Congregationalist minister father and free rein in the household library instilled in Abigail a lifelong "fondness for Reading." As a reader Abigail tended more toward nonfiction than novels and improved her time with history and the classics. As a critic Abigail knew exactly what she liked, what she didn't, and why. Molière's plays, already a century old, sadly disappointed her. "I cannot be brought to like them," she declared to her literary friend

Mercy Otis Warren, herself a playwright. "There seems to me to be a general want of Spirit . . . There are no characters but what appear unfinished and he seems to have ridiculed Vice without engageing us to Virtue . . ."

As a young woman, Abigail's determination to make the most of her self-education prompted John's teasing. "In the Fourth Place you very often hang your Head like a Bulrush," he informed Abigail months before their wedding in a mock catalogue of her defects. "You do not sit, erected as you ought . . . This Fault is the Effect and Consequence of another, still more inexcusable in a Lady. I mean an Habit of reading, Writing and Thinking. But both the Cause and the Effect ought to be repented and amended as soon as possible." For all his teasing, John Adams supported Abigail's commitment to learning, and frequently obliged her requests for books.

Abigail was self-conscious about the unevenness of her spelling and sentence construction throughout her life. Aware of her own limitations, Abigail insisted that her children have the best education she could provide. The war's interference with established schools was a particular trial. "I know not what to do with my children," she wrote in distraction at one point. "We have no Grammer School in the Town, nor have we had for 5 years." Abigail persevered, however, and made other arrangements: a tutor for little John Quincy, school in Boston for thirteen-year-old Nabby, lessons from their minister uncle for young Charley and Tommy. In due time her efforts were rewarded; all three sons were at Harvard by 1786.

For daughters, of course, there were no opportunities for higher education. There were no colleges for women, and male institutions did not accept female students. It was more than a question of practicality. In America before 1800 many people of both sexes accepted the assumption that women were naturally subordinate to men in intellect as in bodily strength.

Abigail Adams believed that men's and women's capabilities and spheres were different; but she could not agree that women were inferior beings. As the eighteenth century drew to a close Abigail and other thoughtful women turned with interest to voices more radical than theirs. One such was Mary Wollstonecraft, an English feminist whose *Vindication of the*

Rights of Women (1792) argued that women were men's equals in intellect and as such deserved equal opportunity for education. Her view was considered extreme.

And that brings us to today. The century that ended the scribblers' eighteenth century, after all, ushered in our own twentieth century. We have vindicated and continue to vindicate Mary Wollstonecraft's ideas. The training that turns sons into lawyers, doctors, clergy, legislators, and published authors is now available to daughters, and mothers too, for that matter. It would seem that we are indeed fulfilling Mercy Warren's exhortation "to be pursuing some mental improvement and yet neglect none of the duties of domestic life."

But how do you do it, I seem to hear the scribblers wonder. Cooking, cleaning, washing, having babies, raising children—how does a woman do all that and something else, besides? Who takes care of the home? (Mercy Warren said it was easy, that all you needed was "a methodical and uniform plan of conduct, united with an industrious mind.")

It's a good question. No doubt some two hundred years hence other eyes will search *our* scribblings for the answers we are finding now.

When I was But a Child my Dear Parents sent me to school
to Mrs. D.W. where there was some Children that I now think
was none of the Cleaverest. I Dont write this to excuse myself
for I know I want sent to Learn of them, But O how ready
I was to idle!

Jemima Condict, age 24   West Orange, New Jersey   1779

If you complain of neglect of Education in sons, What shall
I say with regard to daughters, who every day experience the
want of it. With regard to the Education of my own children,
I find myself soon out of my depth, and destitute and deficient
in every part of Education.

Abigail Adams, age 31   Boston   1776 August 14

*An eighteenth-century schoolgirl portrayed
her academy on this cross-stitched sampler
shortly before 1800.*

I have taken a very great fondness forreading Rollin's ancient
History since you left me. I am determined to go thro with it
if posible in these my days of solitude. I find great pleasure
and entertainment from it, and I have perswaided Johnny to
read me a page or two every day, and hope he will from his
desire to oblige me entertain a fondness for it.

Abigail Adams, age 29   Braintree, Massachusetts   1774 August 19

Tell Mrs. Norton I should like to present my Granddaughters to her sons; They are sprightly lively children. Susan is very forward and intelligent for three years, and would stand all day to hear you read stories ... and has got all goody Goose stories by Heart as her uncle J.Q. Adams did Giles Ginger Bread. She tells me all her Letters and would read in a month if she had a good school.

Abigail Adams, age 54   East Chester, New York   1799 October 31

The morning I left home as I was quitting my chamber the thought that perhaps in the evenings on the road I might wish for a book led me to step back to my bureau, and putting Paradise lost in one pocket, and Charlotte Smiths sonnets in the other ... supplied myself thus inadvertantly with the only books we have here, except a bible ... now I would readily pawn one of my gowns for its worth in books.

Abby May, age 24   Ballston Spa, New York   1800 June 3

This morning, having amply studied my *own* library, I beg'd a volume of any kind from our landlady, she had none, one of her girls offer'd me the vicar of Wakefield, which I thankfully accepted ... so the vicar must amuse me again tomorrow, and next day, and next day, for ought I see!

Abby May, age 24   Ballston Spa, New York   1800 June 3

I have read my bible to my aunt this morning (as is the daily custom) & sometimes I read other books to her. So you may perceive, I *have the use of my tongue* & I tell her it is a good thing to have the use of my tongue.

Nanny Green Winslow, age 12   Boston   1772 February 9

Have taught little Jonathan to read; he learns very fast.

*Martha Ballard, age 60
Augusta, Maine
1795 February 22*

Well, knowledge is a fine thing, and mother Eve thought so; but she smarted so severely for hers, that most of her daughters have been afraid of it since.

*Abigail Adams, age 46
Philadelphia
1791 March 20*

I spent my afternoon in reading the "minister" (a drama of the German Schiller) aloud to a party of Ladies ... I much wish we could oftener form these reading partys—I am oblidged to frequently appear unsociable, for read, and write I will.

Abby May, age 24   Ballston Spa, New York   1800 July 26

My dear niece ...

We have sent your cousins some books, amongst which is Rousseau upon Botany; if you borrow it of them, it will entertain you ... There is also Dr. Priestley upon Air, and Bishop Watson upon Chemistry, all of which are well worth the perusal of minds eager for knowledge and science ... If they are not the amusements which females in general are fond of, it is because trifles are held up to them in a more important light, and no pains taken to initiate them in more rational amusements.

Abigail Adams, age 41   London   1786 July 18

It was the night of the full moon—and never was a more elegant evening. It was an excellent time for frolicking but I can say with sincerity I never once wish'd myself at Broads. I have danced and racketed about so much I have quite lost my relish for it—and spent a much more agreeable evening viewing the moon Jupiter Mars and other of the heavenly bodies thro an excellent telescope which the good Doctr appear'd to take great pleasure in directing and accomodating to our convenience—and answerd our questions with great good humour.

Abigail May, age 20   Portland, Maine   1796 August

But in this country you need not be told how much female Education is neglected, nor how fashonable it has been to ridicule Female learning, tho I acknowled[ge] it my happiness to be connected with a person of a more generous mind and liberal Sentiments.

Abigail Adams, age 33   Braintree, Massachusetts   1778 June 30

Upon the whole I look upon a good education as the greatest of blessing but I think it may be misapplied . . .
    I pity girls that are possess'd of such pleasing qualifications and have such a taste for dress and company to be obliged to live at such a doleful place as New Casco—if their Father had not sent them to Mrs Snows to Portland and allow'd them to read and dress as they chose they might have been happy in a plain garb carding spinning & tending the dairy . . .

Abby May, age 20   Portland, Maine   1796

Very warm
but wet walking.
I have such poor shoes
that I cannot go
to meeten.

Molly Cooper, age 58
Oyster Bay, Long Island
1773 January 27

Did Mr. Chapman Preach a Sermon To Women and this was his text, *many women has done Vertuously but thou Excelest them all.* PROVERBS the 31 C & 29 Verse.

Jemima Condict, age 18   West Orange, New Jersey   1773 April 20

I walked to meeten.
I felt very happy
parte of this day.

Molly Cooper, age 58
Oyster Bay, Long Island
1772 June 7

O, I am trying to fit my cloths to go to meeten in as much distres as my heart can hold. . . . I am forced to get dinner and cannot go to meten atall. Alas, how unhappy and meresabel I am. I feele banished from God and all good.

Molly Cooper, age 54   Oyster Bay, Long Island   1769 March 12

We went by the New Lite meeten and so along til we come to the Quaker meeten house where we went in and heard some poor preaching. O Lord, grant some lite to these poore benighted peopel.

Molly Cooper, age 56   Oyster Bay, Long Island   1771 May 5

Went to old Jerusalem— the Doctr labours hard and shrugs with all his might—but really, and in truth, he is wondrous dull.

Abby May, age 20   Portland, Maine   1796 August

Arise O god and Plead My Cause
O save me by thy Power
if ere I reverence thy Laws
Gide this important hour

.   .   .

Luckless ye kings Its not your right
To heaven it Doth belong
the Race not always to the Swift
Nor Battle to the Strong.

Jemima Condict, age 18   Orange, New Jersey   1773

Mr. Ballard cleaned, planted seed and sowed it. He has seen 75 years. I have bakt and done my other work. O parent allmighty, give me strength to bear all that thou are pleased to lay upon me; and may all things work for good to my immortal soul.

Martha Ballard, age 65   Augusta, Maine   1800 May 17

The Congregationalist ''Old Jerusalem'' meeting house where Abby May heard the ''wondrous dull'' minister in 1796.

Afterword

According to family tradition, Nanny Green Winslow died of tuberculosis in 1779, aged twenty.

⊙

Twenty-four-year-old Jemima Condict married her first cousin Aaron Harrison in the spring of 1779. Jemima died in November; their first and only child, a boy, died in childhood. Aaron later remarried and had four children by his second wife; they named one daughter Jemima.

⊙

Abby May did not recover her health at Ballston Spa in the summer of 1800. She went home to Boston and died in September, aged twenty-four.

⊙

Aunt Bek Dickinson continued to live quietly in Massachusetts and became known as a stead-fast, helpful old soul. She died on the last day of December in 1815, aged seventy-seven.

⊙

Martha Ballard continued delivering babies—only four short of a thousand all told—until a few months before her death in 1812 at age seventy-seven. Martha left over fifty children and grandchildren. Mr. Ballard lived nine years more and died at age ninety-five.

⊙

Three months after her fiftieth wedding anniversary in 1778, Molly Cooper died at age sixty-four; her husband Joseph followed three months later at age seventy-three. Molly and Joseph survived all six of their children.

⊙

Abigail Adams lived for seventy-three years and died in the fall of 1817. Eight years later, her son John Quincy became the nation's sixth President. John Adams survived his wife of over fifty years by nine years, and joined her in death in 1826 on the Fourth of July.

Sources & Acknowledgments

Sources & Acknowledgments

> I have just finished reading a quare of Paper which was
> wrote by me in the year 1771 ... my intent was to burn
> them after thay was looked over thay are wrote and Spelt
> so Poorly that it works me to See them yet I may be glad
> to look them over Some years hence.
>
> *Aunt Bek Dickinson, age 50   Hatfield, Massachusetts   1789 June*

I have preserved the scribblers' original spelling and punctuation as I read them in manuscript or published versions, making slight changes only when the original is unduly confusing.

The *Diary of Anna Green Winslow: A Boston School Girl of 1771* was published with biographical information and extensive annotation by Alice Morse Earle (Boston: Houghton, Mifflin/Riverside Press, Cambridge, 1894).

Jemima Condict's manuscript diary is owned by the New Jersey Historical Society in Newark. I used *Jemima Condict: Her Book* with an introduction by Wilbur Macey Stone (Newark, N.J.: Carteret Book Club, 1930). Excerpts with standardized spelling and punctuation and biographical information appear in *Weathering the Storm: Women of the American Revolution* by Elizabeth Evans (New York: Scribner, 1975.)

Abigail May's 1800 journal, written in Ballston Spa, belongs to the Arthur and Elizabeth Schlesinger Library on the History of Women in America at Radcliffe College. A 1796 journal, written by Abby during a visit to Portland, Maine, is owned by the Maine Historical Society in Portland.

The Maine State Museum in Augusta owns the original diary of Martha Ballard. I used "The Diary of Mrs. Martha Moore Ballard (1785–1812)," published in *The History of Augusta* by Charles Elventon Nash (Augusta, Me.: Charles E. Nash & Son, 1904).

The manuscript diary of Mary ("Molly") Cooper belongs to the Oyster Bay Historical Society in Oyster Bay, New York. I used *The Diary of Mary Cooper: Life on a Long Island*

Farm, 1768–1773 (Oyster Bay Historical Society, 1981), with an introduction and extensive annotation by Field Horne, to whom I am indebted for assistance.

The manuscript diary of Rebecca ("Aunt Bek") Dickinson belongs to the Billings family, descendants of Aunt Bek's sister. I used a transcript in the Pocumtuck Valley Memorial Association in Deerfield, Massachusetts, as well as excerpts with commentary printed as "An Old Maid's Diary" in *The Evening Post* (New York), January 9, 1892.

The original correspondence of Abigail Adams is divided among many collections. I used the 1784–85 Abigail Adams Letters in the collection of the American Antiquarian Society in Worcester, Massachusetts, with thanks to that institution for its gracious assistance.

I also used published versions. *Letters of Mrs. Adams,* the first publication of her correspondence, was edited by Charles Francis Adams, her grandson, who standardized her spelling and punctuation. I used the fourth edition (Boston: Wilkins, Carter, and Company, 1848). *New Letters of Abigail Adams, 1788–1801* (Boston: Houghton Mifflin/Riverside Press, Cambridge, 1947) was edited by Stewart Mitchell, who published the letters precisely as written. For letters before 1784 I used *The Book of Abigail and John: Selected Letters of the Adams Family, 1762–1784* (Cambridge: Harvard University Press, 1975), edited and with an introduction by L. H. Butterfield, Marc Friedlaender, and Mary-Jo Kline. I also used *The Adams–Jefferson Letters: The Complete Correspondence between Thomas Jefferson and Abigail and John Adams,* in two volumes, edited by Lester J. Cappon (Chapel Hill: University of North Carolina Press/Institute of Early American History and Culture at Williamsburg, Virginia, 1959.)

I offer special personal thanks to four people who directly influenced this book. Angus Cameron, my first editor at Knopf, suggested the topic. Alice Quinn, my present editor, brought it to completion with sweet sensitivity. Betty Anderson, the designer, made the book look wonderful. Roma Hansis, friend and colleague, helped me make sense of it; I could not have done it without her suggestions.

Glossary

Glossary

Adams ale	humorous term for water
animal magnetism	another term for mesmerism or hypnotism, popularized by F. A. Mesmer (1734–1815) for treatment of pain
bakt podins	alternative spelling for baked puddings
bell-metal	copper-tin alloy, similar to bronze, for making bells and kettles
blisters	anything applied to raise a blister, supposed to draw off sickness from the body
blocktin	a form of tin
box	in this sense, leaves from the box shrub, used for decoration
cambrick	a kind of fine white linen
chairs	a form of transportation; an enclosed sedan chair for one person, carried on poles by two men
chemise, chimise	a stylish loose gown worn by women, similar to a shift
cherry bounce	cherry liqueur
chip chapeau	a hat or bonnet woven of thin strips of wood or woody fiber

cittel	alternative spelling for kettle
cocumberries	berries from the East Indian cocum tree, from which a yellow-green oil or butter is produced
demi-saison	*robe de demi-saison,* a dress, intermediate between winter and summer wear
dominie	alternative spelling for domino, a fashionable loose cloak
draws	alternative spelling for drawers, or underpants
floor cloth	sturdy painted canvas or oilcloth floor covering, like linoleum, popular in the eighteenth century
fortans	alternative spelling for fortunes
gauze	very thin transparent fabric of silk, cotton, or linen
gill	a quarter pint
harslett	alternative spelling for haslet, or organ meats, including heart, liver, etc.
hatchel	to dress flax with a metal-toothed comb
heshling	alternative spelling for hatcheling
hogshead	a large cask
hough	alternative spelling for hoe

lappets	streamers on a woman's cap, bonnet, or headdress
lawn	a kind of fine linen
lutestring	glossy silk fabric
mangoes	another term for pickles, especially of melon or cucumber
mantuamaker	dressmaker
neet's feet	alternative spelling for neat's foot, or the foot of an ox used as food
panniers	large baskets slung across the back of a beast of burden for carrying provisions
past pin	alternative spelling for paste pin, or pin with artificial gemstones
pearl ash	a kind of baking powder introduced in the late eighteenth century as an alternative to yeast
planthorn	probably a horn of plenty
plurisy	alternative spelling for pleurisy, an illness causing difficult breathing and coughing
pompedore	alternative spelling for pompadour, fabric either a shade of pink or printed in a flower-sprig pattern; named for the Marquise de Pompadour (1721–64), mistress of Louis XV
puter	alternative spelling for pewter

rout	a large party or reception
rusk	dry, crisp sweet bread or cake
sack	alternative spelling for sacque, a fashionable French style of gown with a pleated train falling from the shoulders in the back
salute	to greet with a kiss
sauches	alternative spelling for sausage
sause	alternative spelling for sauce, commonly used to mean fruits and vegetables or produce in general
spirit	distilled alcoholic beverage
sponge	in baking, the light, spongy batter formed by mixing yeast with a small measure of flour; more flour is then added to rise and form the full batch of dough
swingle	wooden blade used to beat and clean flax fibers
syllabub	a sweet, frothy milk drink
tiffany	thin, transparent silk fabric
travail	another term for women's labor in childbirth
wedners	alternative spelling for weddingers, or the wedding party and guests

NOTES ABOUT THE DRAWINGS
THAT INTRODUCE EACH CHAPTER

page 2   Diagram showing how to make a quill pen.

page 14   A popular emblem imprinted on such things as teapots and handkerchiefs, exhorting eighteenth-century women to "Keep within Compass."

page 28   Common tableware: wooden dishes, pewter porringer and spoon, and bone-handled knife.

page 44   Garden equipment: a wrought-iron spade and hoe, wooden rake, harvest basket, and "watering pott." The fence kept out wild or barnyard animals.

page 66   An alphabet of the initials used for marking linens and clothing. I and J were often used interchangeably, but whoever made it forgot the F!

page 84   A quilting frame with quilting pattern. Holes and pegs allowed the women to adjust the frame as work progressed.

page 100   Medicinal herbs.

page 118   A woman's writing desk with brass pulls, c. 1800.

A NOTE ABOUT THE AUTHOR

June Sprigg, the author of By Shaker Hands,
is a writer and illustrator who lives in Pittsfield, Massachusetts.
Her interest in diaries and artifacts relating to womens' lives
grew from graduate studies in early American culture
at the Henry Francis Du Pont Winterthur Museum in Delaware.
She is currently at work on an illustrated book
based on women's diaries from the Oregon
and California trails, circa 1850.

A NOTE ON THE TYPE

The text of this book was composed in a film version of Palatino,
a typeface designed by the noted German typographer Hermann Zapf.
Named after Giovanbattista Palatino, a writing master of Renaissance Italy,
Palatino was the first of Zapf's typefaces to be introduced in America.
The first designs for the face were made in 1948,
and the fonts for the complete face were issued between 1950 and 1952.
Like all Zapf-designed typefaces, Palatino is
beautifully balanced and exceedingly readable.

Composition by Centennial Graphics,
Ephrata, Pennsylvania.
Printing and binding by The Murray Printing Company,
Westford, Massachusetts.
Calligraphy by G. G. Laurens
Design by Betty Anderson